NetWorking Success

How to Turn Business & Financial Relationships into Fun & Profit

Anne Boe
Author of *Is Your Net-Working?*

Health Communications, Inc.
Deerfield Beach, Florida

Library of Congress Cataloging-in-Publication Data

Boe, Anne, (date)
    Networking success : how to turn business & financial relationships
into fun & profit / Anne Boe.
      p.   cm.
    Includes index.
    Originally published: Encintas, Calif. : Seaside Press, 1994.
    ISBN 1-55874-365-0 (trade paper) : $12.95
    1. Success in business. 2. Strategic alliances (Business) 3. Inter-
organizational relations. 4. Social networks. I. Title.
HF5386.B592 1995
650.1'3--dc20   95-42819
                                                   CIP

© 1994 Anne Boe
ISBN 1-55874-365-0

Publisher: Health Communications, Inc.
          3201 S.W. 15th Street
          Deerfield Beach, Florida 33442-8190

Cover design by Luke Pham

I dedicate this book to all my special, loving, healing friends and teachers who have enhanced my life, spirit and ability to love and receive. Through their generous energy gifts, my life has become special and extremely meaningful. As a result of all their teachings, I am into creating a new networking game! In special appreciation I want to name Pila, Mark Victor Hansen, Reverend Celesta Meola, Reverend John Logan and Bob Easter. My thanks and gratitude to each one of these people for sharing their love and light with me and for being such wonderful, loyal networking friends.

CONTENTS

FOREWORD by Mark Victor Hansen   *ix*

ACKNOWLEDGMENTS   *xi*

INTRODUCTION   1

Chapter 1 *JUMP START YOUR*
           NETWORKING!   7

Chapter 2 *NETWORKING IS AN*
           INSIDE JOB!   31

Chapter 3 *A COMMUNITY OF*
           COMMUNICATION   65

Chapter 4 *NETWORKING CHANGES*
           YOUR FUTURE!   103

Chapter 5 *MANAGING YOUR*
           NETWORK   149

Chapter 6 *NETWORKING FOR*
           NETWORTHING   177

Chapter 7 *NETWORKING NOTABLES*   203

FOREWORD

Anne Boe's personality mimics that of champagne bubbles. She is sparkling wine in human form. When you get in her energy orbit, she immediately enrolls you in conversation and in her beloved passion, vocation, and avocation—networking—the purposeful gathering of two or more people for fun, love, business, and life.

Anne is the first lady of networking. Like the famous James Bond theme song says: 'Nobody does it better . . . .' No one networks or teaches networking half as well as Anne. She does such a magnificent job that I have hired her to talk and teach at my seminars in California and Hawaii—to many of the most powerful and influential leaders in the world. Every attendee automatically falls in love with Anne—her ideas, networking strategies and the obvious new results they achieve by employing her principles.

At our last annual Transformation Intensive Seminar in Kona, Hawaii, a man who owns the largest real estate company in Austin, Texas and his wife, a top IBM executive, caught Anne's vision, substance and style. They were so enchanted and captivated by the way she geometrically expanded their possibilities, that they wrote her a 12-page testimonial thank-you letter outlining all their breakthroughs due to her sage insights and romantic verbal picturing of what's possible.

I love networking. I use it daily for the benefit and betterment of my world, my business, my clients, my family and myself. Networking has provided me a life and lifestyle that is magnificent, complete, meaningful and omnibeneficial. Anne's wisdom in this book can do the same or more for you!

If everyone knew how to network successfully, we could truly enter a Golden Age of abundance, peace and plenty for all. We'd cooperate rather than compete. We could make the world a place of absolute success, joy and bliss for total humanity.

One last note: when Anne arrived at our Hawaii seminar in August of 1993, she looked gaunt, thin, pale, ill, weak and as though her time on earth was reaching a climax. I asked her what was wrong. She said that she had terminal colon cancer.

I told Anne what a colleague, Deepak Chopra, aureudic medical doctor from India, has said, "If anyone has ever overcome a terminal disease, [then] potentially everyone with a terminal disease can overcome it."

"Better yet," I said to Anne, "we have 16 chiropractors, four Reiki Healers, a superb reflexologist and a Filipino faith healer in attendance—all willing to serve you if you're vulnerable enough to share your problem and be open to new solutions. Besides, after you speak, I'll lead a healing experience dedicated to you, and the entire audience will ensconce you in loving, healing, energy—if you okay it." As a networker willing to be open and grow through her own problems, she agreed. By Friday, she announced that she had no more pain and no more symptoms. She checked it out with a medical doctor and found out that she was cancer free.

As human beings, we all encounter real big-time problems physically, mentally, emotionally, financially, spiritually and in our relationships. We each need to be able to network effectively in the sweet now-and-now to get results like Anne has, does and will continue to get.

It is my heartfelt recommendation that you devour this book. Hand it to the person(s) with whom you most want to network. After you ingest, digest and own these ideas, principles, skills and techniques, use them to make your world and our world better off in every way.

—Mark Victor Hansen
Author of *Chicken Soup for the Soul* and *The Master Motivator,*
networker, professional speaker and successful entrepreneur.

ACKNOWLEDGMENTS

Over the past 13 years I have traveled the United States, Canada, Singapore and Sydney, Australia speaking on the power of networking. I never realized how vital my message was to heal my own inner power and self-worth. As my keynote, motivational speaking and writing business continue to soar and expand, I am thankful to many who have contributed love, guidance and support. I am grateful to Lia Keep and Rosemary Readman for letting me share my networking message to all the Weekenders Casual Wear people. A special thanks to Mark Victor Hansen for including me in his Kona, Hawaii transformational workshop. I realized I obtained a tremendous amount of healing and new insights as a result of this intensive week.

To Ilona Eve for her healing touch and gifts, to George Roman Beverly Hills psychic astrologer for his wisdom, business insights and unending love and kindness. To Doug Shaw and C. Bailey for their continued support and appreciation of my work to the National Management Association for over eight years. A very special honor and tribute to my dear friend Diane O'Brien for her editing talents and time put into this book. She has the finest integrity and commitment that an author can ever hope for. To Elaine Winter for her loyal friendship and support through the Council of Logistics Management. To Cabett Robert for always supporting and inspiring me to greatness in my speaking to the National Speakers Association. To Jamie Ariza and Mike Hamilton at John Wiley and Sons, Inc. for believing and supporting my networking ideas and all of my writing. To Wynn Topley at Pepsi Cola in Chicago for understanding and living my message. A very special thank you to my great friend and Sydney, Australia networker, Robyn Henderson for her magnificent work and great talent. To my friend Susan Tofteland for her dedicated friendship and networking ideas. To San Diego Convention and Visitors Bureau and the San Diego Business Journal for supporting me with my doing seminars and all the many articles they have written about me throughout the years of my business. To Randy Dunn for being there for me in such an unconditional loving way, and I also acknowledge my mother Lenore Weis and the wonderful loving memory of my father, Milton Weis for their support in always allowing me to be the free-spirited entrepreneur that I creatively became. To all these wonderful people and all of you who sent me thank-you notes, cards, love calls, a special tribute for honoring me and for being willing to share your energy. Remember, we are all in this networking game together!!

INTRODUCTION

"We are all in this together!"

Congratulations! If you feel as though you have been attending the "school of hard knocks," I have great news for you. Your life is going to change—for the better! This is the day you begin to learn how networking can turn your life around. Above all it is fun, and it works for you if you work at it!

This networking book is to help you, the reader, open up to the possibilities of mutual achievement through the positive aspects of helping each other grow in the future, if not immediately. We need to help each other and we need each other's help. The best way to teach is by example. Through learning, practicing and making a commitment to networking, you can be a model for others and can eliminate the misconceptions and abusive uses of networking. Networking can be a powerful, positive experience of goodwill, trust, service, contribution and joy!

After reviewing the last 12 years of being in the network business as a motivational keynote speaker in the United States and internationally, I am in awe at the growth in the networking industry. Now it is the "in thing" to be a networker. When I began my speaking business, I could not use the word "networking" in the title of my speech because the topic was too vague to be of concern for many groups of people.

Times have changed, and people are creating the success and prosperity they deserve. Networking is alive and thriving.

Networking is not a fad—it is definitely here to stay. Everyday, successful people are discovering that networking is a business skill that can help reduce their workload, increase productivity and even lead to the start-up of other networks and new relationships.

After much success with my book, *Is Your Net-Working?* published by John Wiley & Sons, Inc., 1989, there was an overwhelming response and desire for more information. This response led to the creation of this book. I have incorporated a "hands on" approach to share with you my dynamic, on-going process of networking principles, skills and techniques. This networking book is really a workbook—no, a funbook—about the adventure of meeting the most important living person in the world. That person is you. You will explore your interaction with others, your goals, your aspirations, your dreams and how you feel about your life. By the time you finish this book you will not only know yourself more intimately, but you will be able to approach networking with ease and enthusiasm. Once you start practicing these principles and rules, you will discover that networking easily fits into your lifestyle. You will be getting what you want from life, your career and relationships, and you will be meeting your goals.

Although networking has been around as long as people have needed to barter, it is not an instant magic formula for success. Unfortunately, no such formula exists—there's no such thing as an overnight success. Some may claim that they have an instant formula for success, but don't believe it! There is NO QUICK FIX! What I can share with you in this book are ideas on how networking can become a constant integrative technique or an ongoing process toward success. There are critical guidelines, principles and rules that I believe are the foundation of the essential skills for networking. These guidelines include a variety of examples, exercises and affirmations. I encourage you to actively participate to learn how to be successful. The greatest secret of success is: success has no secrets.

Before you start your networking you should know why you should be networking. The reasons will vary depending upon your needs and the nature of the event; whether it is an office conference, a cocktail party, a board meeting or even a parent/teachers meeting.

You should have a clear purpose for attending, and before you attend, ask yourself what you would like to accomplish professionally and personally. Remember that both business and social events can do wonders for your success. In my presentations, I request the audience to list what they feel are the most important personal and professional benefits of networking. The following points are made most often:

1. Freedom of expression: You will be perceived as having confidence, self-esteem and self-control in personal and professional situations.
2. There will be no limits on the amount of gained insight and new information.
3. Increased business/personal contacts.
4. Enhanced career opportunities.
5. Increased invitations and FUN!

HOW TO GET THE MOST FROM THIS BOOK

Read this book from beginning to end. Do not skip any of the lessons. They were arranged in deliberate order to assist you in making a gradual transition from the person you are today to the person that you can be. The first chapter is a discussion of networking itself, so that you will understand what it is that you are getting into. In chapter two you will work on your "self" and the proper attitude and focus that will allow you the flexibility and confidence to excel. Chapter three concentrates on the skills for your interaction with others, and is followed by chapter four with attention on how you can use your newfound skills to fulfill your career aspirations. Tips on managing your networking activities are presented in chapter five, including ways that you can monitor and fine tune your efforts. Prosperity is the focus of chapter six, showing you that you can have anything that you want in your life. Finally, in chapter seven I'll share with you some insight from other master networkers because, after all, isn't that what networking is all about?

HOW DO YOU EAT AN ELEPHANT?

Have you heard the riddle, "How do you eat an elephant?" The
reply is, "In small bites!" You may want to assimilate the ideas presented in this book a little bit at a time. Don't hurry through it
because you may miss something—but also don't procrastinate.
Marvelous things happen when you take action that will put your
subconscious mind to work.

Don't fall into the trap of reading this book in the same casual
style that applies to fiction. Focus on acquiring the tools necessary
for success. A solution is to have a pen or pencil in your hand whenever you open this book. When you read a line or paragraph that is
meaningful to you—underline it! This simple act will greatly
increase your retention of the thought or principle, and make it
easier for you to find it in the future. Participate in all the exercises
and answer with your heart. Remember, this is not a test—there are
no right or wrong answers!

Do you have a pen or pencil in your hand? Fill in your name:

I,_____
can achieve as much wealth and success as I desire, as long as I can
integrate my given talents with newly-acquired knowledge. I will
pay the price with time and effort. I will help others to create a
win-win situation. I understand that success without happiness is
worthless. Success is within me and I am ready to accept it.

Now that's a great beginning! Use this Networking Guide as a
creative method for knowing yourself intimately. This will lead to
mastering the skills of networking. Although networking can be
practiced and improved constantly, the goal of this book is to help
you quickly acquire the skills to increase your networking abilities.
By participating in the exercises you will develop skills that will
help make networking a comfortable, pleasant, profitable and even
enjoyable experience.

Throughout this book you will see "☑BOE'S GUIDES." These
are designed for you to practice the steps that lead to self-confidence
and conviction. Understand them, as they are designed to help you

gain a mastery of communication. By using these guides, you will develop skills that will become your tools to create "customized" networking adventures. This is the essence of what this book is about. The way you communicate with yourself and with others will ultimately determine the quality of your life.

People who succeed in life are those who welcome the challenges of life. They communicate that experience to themselves (speaking with conviction and listening from within) in a way that causes them to successfully change their environment toward that which they desire. Will you agree with me on that? I hope so, because the whole point of this book is that your skills, intuition, knowledge and initiative are the essence of what makes you great. These qualities can be expanded and intensified if you are willing to invest time, effort and money into yourself. Is there any better investment than yourself? Most of us know that there isn't, but many of us don't act often enough or decisively enough on that belief.

Now then, let's begin our networking adventure with curiosity, energy and truthfulness to yourself. Let your emotions flow, and let your desires come to the forefront as you map out your strategy to achieve all that you deserve in your life.

1
JUMP-START YOUR NETWORKING!

*"Networking is mutual desire to share
the joy of giving and the joy of receiving."*

Have you ever said, "The hardest thing is just getting started?" There may be times when we feel it would take a bolt of lightning to jolt us into making changes in our life. By picking up this book, you are obviously not awaiting a bolt of lightning. Perhaps this book is just the little spark you need to motivate you to see how networking can fit into your personal and professional life.

BEWARE OF MYTHS

Networking Success: How to Turn Business and Financial Relationship Into Fun and Profit, gets you ready for your "jump-start" by first shattering cherished, time-wasting myths. Before we start, you need to realize the fallacy of the following major myths of networking:

MYTH: PEOPLE ARE BORN WITH NETWORKING SKILLS

Networking consists of "people skills" that are not a right of birth. They need to be constantly developed. Networking can be accomplished by anyone, anywhere, anytime. High achievement is not possessed by someone blessed with superior intelligence, special skills, an exceptional formal education, or even good luck. Hard work, of and by itself, is not a crucial factor for getting results, taking action, and believing in yourself. Networking does involve some risks and can be learned by anyone! That is, anyone willing and ready to put forth the necessary effort can become a master at learning and practicing these techniques until they become everyday habits.

MYTH: ONE MUST HAVE ACCESS TO THE MYSTERIOUS GUARDED SECRETS OF CLUBS, GROUPS, OR ORGANIZATIONS

Have you ever thought that a network wasn't for you because you thought networking involved some type of exclusive club? Networking is more than just belonging. In the past there were many more exclusive organizations and clubs. They not only had a network, they were well aware that networking was a strategy that had to be played to succeed. One would have to know the players and the proper moves.

Networking is now more than just a game for a few select players. We are all in this together. We need to help each other. It is no longer an exclusive group issue; it is for all people. We need to enhance our communication skills; the ability to create, support, and use relationship skills that require style and substance. The exclusive network is elitist; the new network philosophy is egalitarian. Our economic and emotional survival depends on our networking skills.

MYTH: I CAN MANAGE MY OWN LIFE, I DON'T NEED HELP

There is a notion in our culture that we are supposed to be superhuman beings who can accomplish major feats on our own, never asking for help, and without showing any sign of difficulty. There is no such being as a "self-made" person. Those who have truly earned the world's respect and admiration for their outstanding accomplishments are always quick to point out the many helping hands throughout their life that had helped them to reach the pinnacle. It's time to give up being a lone ranger!

As children, we are taught to obtain values and strengths by becoming independent. If taken properly, this step should have led us to a more powerful stage of inner strength and interdependence. You do not live in a vacuum nor can you harvest the better fruits of life without help and encouragement from others. As a member of a wide human society, your growth depends, to a large degree, on how well you handle your contacts with those who cross your path every hour of the day. Without friendship and assistance the successes you enjoy will be few, if any.

What are your preconceived notions and beliefs about networking?

BOE'S DEFINITION OF NETWORKING

All through history, this powerful skill has served self-created groups of people that share a need or an interest. Networking is an invaluable technique that anyone can use consistantly for building contacts with people to share anything that is mutually beneficial. My definition: "Networking is the process of developing and nurturing personal and professional contacts to obtain 1) referrals, 2) advice, 3) information, 4) support, and 5) energy."

While you may not receive all five benefits of networking from each person with whom you associate, you will receive what you need at the time to meet your goals. As an example, your network can be your safety net, your moral support, and your backup system when you make a job transition, move to a new city, start your own business, change career paths, or most often, when you decide to improve or expand your business. You can also use your network to make new friends and develop more interests. If you are looking for a solution to a business challenge you most likely will network with someone who will provide advice and support. On the other hand, if you are investigating a career change, you will network with the intent of receiving all five benefits.

☑ BOE'S GUIDE #1: Networking is the ability to relate and talk
to anyone, anytime, anywhere. This does not mean interchanges
such as, "Hi, how are you" or "Have a nice day." You, and
everyone you meet, want sincerity and true interest in each other.
If you are going to generate positive communication momentum,
you have to develop an attitude of caring about others and adding
value. When you project this attitude, you are committing yourself
to putting networking into action. Be friendly in a genuine way.
Remember to say what you mean and mean what you say. Honesty
builds trusting relationships.

During one of my recent seminars in San Diego, "Networking
for Your Business, Financial, and Relationship Success," one of my
seminar attendees said, "Anne, we are very worried about you. We
want to start a group to address your predicament." Of course, I
asked, "And what group would that be?" They answered,
"Networkers Anonymous—we think your addicted!" Right on! I
even practice networking at the grocery store, constantly looking for
opportunities to strike up conversations! I start at the oranges,
opening up to whoever is near. If no one talks to me, I move to the
pears. If still no one talks to me, I leave for I am not having fun! I
have even laminated business cards for those times when I am in my
Jacuzzi, as I choose to never miss a networking opportunity!

Networking is a way of life. Once you get into your inner joy
and inner peace, you will never stop. The greatest joy is contribution. The first person you have to contribute to is you. If you leave
yourself out of the equation, you will never be satisfied. You might
have all the riches and outer trappings, but you will never feel
good about you. Networkers know how to combine their feelings
and their intellect so that they always create win-win, long term
relationships. Networkers always stay within their integrity and
never give up.

☑ BOE'S GUIDE #2: Networking is the art of creating momentum
towards what you want. Networkers have a tendency to go towards
what they don't want and, believe it or not, it takes more energy
to be negative than to be positive. This negative momentum is

perpetuated by doubts ("I would, but . . ."), insecurity ("I'm not sure that . . ."), or the lack of definitive goals ("Well, maybe . . ."). Negative energy is stronger than positive energy. The mere dwelling on anything negative is virtually guaranteed to make it become reality. If you think you may fail, you will fail. So don't think it! Don't devote one second to negativity or ignore it, either, if you feel it creeping into your thoughts. You must overcome negativity and never allow it to persist. Address it as something that you acknowledge but won't tolerate, and then change your thoughts and behaviors toward a more positive attitude. Only think and act toward what you want.

It may be difficult, but it is a good practice to think ahead and ask yourself what you truly want in your life. Knowing what you want is the starting point to knowing where you want to be in five years. What do you want in the next six months? Then envision your needs in three years, two years, and then next year. What can I do for my own career networking today to further my career success?

BENEFITS OF NETWORKING

Everyone deserves to have everything they want. One of the best things in life is to be content and happy about your professional and personal life. You will learn more about others and their successes, what works and what doesn't, what career opportunities are available and what paths are good for you. No one limits your growth but you. If you want to earn more, learn more and increase your competence. Stay in touch with you.

Life is a constant journey of learning. You will discover what you need, to enjoy successful networking. You will learn the skills you need to learn, why you need to learn them, and how you can learn them. Best of all, these skills never can be taken from you—even under the most adverse circumstances. Once you've acquired these skills, you're always able to pick yourself up and quickly start moving in the right direction. It is interesting to hear how networking has changed the direction of those who have made it a way of life. You will rise above the little irritations and begin to experience the greatness of your life.

Here are some success tips for networking:

The most important benefit of networking is the advancement of day-to-day business productivity, efficiency, and achievement. You can and will achieve your career dreams.

When networking is sincere, genuine, and not self-serving, it can be quite powerful. I can't imagine where I would be today if I didn't use these networking principles.

Depending upon advice and information has been important in advancing my career. I know the value of listening is an important networking tool.

Real winners are those who make networking a part of their nature. It all begins by unconditionally loving yourself and others. When you live and give in this way you will receive back more than you expected.

Working alone is too restrictive. Networking brings balance and enjoyment into your life.

Networking depends on focusing your energy. Networking then becomes fun and profitable. My philosophy is that if it's not fun, it's not worth doing!

Networking is rewarding. You'll feel good when you know you're helping people, and often receive more than you give. Expect the unexpected!

I owe my good fortune to meeting others through networking. Amazing things started to happen when I finally realized what I really wanted. Once I knew what I wanted, I started letting others know my wants and desires! Results happened quickly. Now, every day I awake with wonderful anticipation!

Results were astonishing as I extended networking to community involvement and activities. Everyone wanted to help me!

In the business of selling, trust is very important. It makes a sale much easier! A referral is worth it's weight in gold! Take time to build trust slowly.

As I was making a list of those whom I would like to have attend my last birthday party, I realized that one of the best benefits of networking was developing a base of wonderful friends. I can then take more risks and tackle things I normally wouldn't attempt. It helps my self-confidence to know that I have a backup system or safety net if I ever need help. Everything is not life or death! What's not to like about networking? I'm building bridges to help me become as successful as I would like to be. I'm creating new business, feeling good about myself, and enjoying other people.

Can you list additional benefits of networking?

_____

_____

_____

_____

_____

List your networking areas needing improvement and resolve to work on them.

_____

_____

_____

_____

_____

THE RIGHT WAY TO NETWORK

Many people assume that the networking game must be 'played' to succeed. They believe it to be coercing or manipulating, not networking as we know and define it in the "giving without expectation" definition. Today networking is more than a game—it is a method of joint communication and mutual benefit. As Anthony Putman emphasizes in *Marketing Your Services* (1990, p. 171), "The purpose of networking is to give and get information. If you use networking properly nobody feels pressured, used, or put on the spot. You are not selling, you are telling. You are not asking for favors, you are giving valuable information." People naturally want to support each other, especially when trust and respect are present in a relationship. When people trust each other, they will do the best they can, reciprocate when they can, and serve you in the same way that they have been served. Networkers "get together to get ahead." Your career, survival, and prosperity depend on your networking skills.

BUILDING A FOUNDATION OF RELATIONSHIPS

Networking is building foundations of relationships that are mutually supportive and empowering. Use resources around you by gathering and distributing information, ideas and contacts. When you are networking, you and all of your contacts are benefiting. You are building the net of connections that provide the foundation for all of your future endeavors. It's about the success, accomplishments, and confidence of working with others, and about putting people together to get results. It's all about self-nurturing and enjoying your new found freedom.

CORPORATE AMERICA STARTS NETWORKING

Corporations are realizing the value of networking, especially in today's competitive business environment. I have experienced this in the growth of my speaking business. More and more I see that networking is a vital, vibrant, growing area of business that more companies are incorporating into their outline for success. It's a necessary process that enhances the quality of work and enriches the relationships that are a part of the work place. Corporate America is now realizing that information is power when it is exchanged. More and more corporations are encouraging their employees to communicate and connect with professional and personal networks. What you don't know can be a detriment.

Have you noticed employees who are getting ahead and having more fun doing it? Those who "live networking" know that they will attain success with greater ease, joy, and efficiency. Most importantly, they know the right way to approach networking. They practice daily the game plan, rules, and rituals. They know their direction, examine their purpose and parlay their position to benefit their career, company, and community. They make a difference. Charles Kettering of General Motors shows the passion for work he expects from his employees by stating the following:

> I tell my people that I don't want any fellow who has a job working for me; what I want is a fellow whom a job has. And I want the job to get a hold on this young man so hard that no matter where he is, the job has got him for keeps. I want that job to have him in its clutches when he goes to bed at night, and in the morning I want that job to be siting at the foot of the bed telling him, 'It's time to get up and go to work!' And when a job gets a fellow that way, he's sure to amount to something.

TRAITS OF NETWORKERS

I am always intrigued by the variety of networkers' backgrounds, the diversity of their personalities, and the range of their interests. And yet they have many traits in common, foremost of which is the degree of their clarity, focus, wisdom, and acceptance. They know exactly what they are doing and where they are going. This book, like my seminars, is directed at helping you learn how to achieve this clarity, focus, and wisdom. By learning and practicing the skills of networking, you will be developing your relationships to attain a new level of productivity, success, and pleasure in your personal and professional life.

Some of the key traits that successful networkers have in common are:

Goals. Networkers do not hesitate to make BIG goals. The bigger the goal, the bigger the reward. They understand that knowing what they want is the starting point for determining what is needed to get what they want. Greatness comes to those who develop a burning desire to achieve BIG goals.

Enjoyment. Successful people enjoy their work. Networkers are having the time of their lives. They work with total involvement toward their goals and are often paid well.

Confidence. Networkers have a positive attitude and plenty of confidence. The successful never seem to doubt that they will succeed. When they do succeed, it contributes to their self-esteem. Networkers expect to win.

Integrity. Successful networkers have integrity and help others to succeed. There is a tendency to develop win-win situations. Networkers are careful to ensure that both sides are happy when deals are made. This is an integral part of success.

Work. The only place that success comes before work is in the dictionary! For example, Thomas Edison tried more than ten thousand experiments before he developed a successful incandescent lamp. He kept searching for something more until he found it. Success is achieved and maintained by those who keep on trying.

Risk. Everyone knows that to succeed, there are times when one has to take risks. There are times when successful people make mistakes, but they shrug them off, learn from those mistakes, and then go on with their lives. To these successful networkers, the rewards outnumber the risks and they enjoy attaining prosperity with greater ease and joy.

Communication. Networkers know to ask for what they want or need. When they come across a problem, they actively seek suggestions from others. They have enough strength to ask for help.

People. Networkers surround themselves with competent, responsible, and supportive people. No matter how smart or creative a person might be, he or she must have others who are trustworthy. These individuals have learned how to be effective by using their surrounding resources and support systems.

Health. It is important to be healthy, have high energy levels and schedule time to renew your energy. This revitalization is so important to successful networkers, they conscientiously schedule time for activities or rest that will help them feel energized again.

Contribution. No matter how busy they are, successful networkers are willing to give of themselves to help a colleague in need, or become involved in political, cultural, or artistic causes.

Practice. To become an expert achiever in any area of life, it

takes practice, practice, and then, more practice along with determination and a sense of self-worth.
Higher Power or Luck. Networkers don't take all the credit
for their successes. For example, many will say, "I just happened
to be at the right place at the right time." True networkers say,
"Thank you for helping me succeed."

☑ BOE'S GUIDE #3: Our attitudes shape our future. Everyone
deserves to live their life to the fullest. Putting positive attitudes
into action can be just the motion to make an incredible difference
in your personal and professional life. If you know what you want,
you are more apt to recognize it when you see it. When you read
a book, for example, you will recognize information that will help
you get what you want.

In these times you still have your personal right to say: "This
is what I want most to accomplish." You have everything to gain
and nothing to lose by trying. To many, the riches of life can be
quite different. Success is obtaining skills in day-to-day living
which results in a happy, love-filled life. You can have these and
other riches, too. The choice is yours.

With this attitude of wanting and deserving to live your life to
the fullest, you will discover a power that leads to a richer fuller
personal and professional life. When Henley wrote the poetic lines,
"I am the master of my fate, I am the captain of my soul," he could
have informed us that we are the masters of our fate because we
are in control of our attitudes.

Remember, attitudes can be constructive or destructive. By
having positive thoughts and attitudes, we can translate those thoughts
into reality. When our attitude towards ourselves is generous and
merciful, we attract big and generous portions of success. Be careful
to never underestimate the power of negative attitudes. If our
attitudes are negative we can attract despair and defeat.

"You are your best friend. Your success, health, happiness,
and wealth depend upon your positive thoughts and attitudes."
To be successful in life, it is imperative to have a positive

attitude by adopting and applying several principles in your daily life. Analyze yourself courageously and learn which of these principles you are using and which of them you have been neglecting:

One of my mental attitudes is: _____

_____

_____

What I want most is: _____

_____

_____

I focus my thinking towards: _____

_____

_____

What is likable about my personality is: _____

_____

_____

I am enthusiastic about: _____

_____

_____

I am a good team player because: _____

_____

_____

I am budgeting my time and money for: _____

_____

_____

I am keeping in good physical health by: _____

_____

_____

I am keeping in good mental health by: _____

_____

_____

I am demonstrating good listening skills by: _____

_____

_____

I am able to plan by: _____

_____

_____

I am showing self-discipline by: _____

_____

_____

I am contributing by: _____

_____

_____

My creative life vision is: _____

_____

_____

I am generous with: _____

_____

My belief in a higher power is: _____

_____

☑ BOE'S GUIDE #4: Knowing and asking for what you want can make a major difference in obtaining success quickly. The main reason people do not network is fear of rejection. I have developed the opposite fear—fear that I might miss you! The first step in getting what you want is setting goals. When you clearly know what you want, you will have great relationships.

A networking example: As soon as I finish keynoting a national or international convention, I send a thank-you note to my meeting planner. Within ten days I call the planner and ask for responses on my presentation. I then ask to schedule the following year with a topic upgrade. Eighty-five percent (85%) of the time I am invited back! This is possible because I had the courage to ask for what I wanted. I always recommend that you believe in yourself and your abilities.

LET OTHERS KNOW WHAT YOU WANT!

Do you feel differently when you use the word need? Wants and needs are separate substances. Wants can appear to be frivolous, hopeful, and many times not taken as seriously as a need. A need appears to be more urgent, meaningful, worthy, and not as capricious as a want. For example:

People want big expensive cars; they need transportation.
People want prestige; they need respect.
People want ease and comfort; they need achievement and work.

YOUR WANTS, YOUR NEEDS

☑ BOE'S GUIDE #5: When you give others what they need, they will give you what you need. The better you are at networking, the more you give to others—your business associates, your family, the economy. Remember, networking consists of creating links with people we know in an organized way, for a specific purpose of sharing and adding value while expecting nothing in return. If you can get things done with people in joy and harmony, helping them grow and becoming more than they ever have been before, then you have one of the most treasured talents anyone can possess. Giving such a gift allows you to receive the best of material and emotional benefits, and to get in return the things that you want. Keep learning to give the gift of acknowledgment.

You may be thinking it was difficult enough to decide what it is that you want, and now I am asking you to find out what other people want! Not only will you need to find out what they want but it will then be your mission to help them get it! When you start incorporating the philosophy of helping others, there will be the realization of the power that comes from an inner strength as you balance and integrate dreams and goals with the people and opportunities around you.

Who are important people in your life?

_____

_____

_____

_____

_____

_____

What are their needs?

_____

_____

_____

_____

_____

What will you do to increase happiness and value in their life?

_____

_____

_____

_____

_____

LOVING ME IS LOVING YOU

If you asked, "What is the greatest yearning within every human being?" the response most likely would be LOVE. Your empathy for others shows your capacity for love. In his book, *University of Success*, Robert Conklin says it so well when he describes love as follows:

> Love is the mainspring of the heart. It is the meaning, the joy, the valleys and the mountains of being. Love freshens the body, nourishes the soul, shapes the spirit, and glorifies the mind. It is the laughter of the heart, the sunrise of each moment. Above all else love is an emotion. That's why it is so vital to the pulse of life. For people are emotional beings. Everything they do is shaped by their emotions.

When you talk with others, note their differences—their uniqueness. See that the differences are not bad—just different. Appreciate those characteristics as the things that make the person unique, and then love that person for being who they are. This will help you more easily understand and accept your own differences, acknowledge who you are and what makes you unique and lovable. Accepting others begins with accepting you.

Can you name some things about you that people would find different or unique?

_____

_____

_____

_____

☑ BOE'S GUIDE #6: Successful people live networking! Networking is a universal principle that is in motion all around the world, evolving from the bartering traditions in ancient civilizations. Through the ages, the power of networking has not depended on age, educational degree, financial status, career path, or geographic preference. The power of networking is available to anyone who is willing to tap their inner resources while working wisely with their outer resources: networks!

Networking becomes a part of your life as you express your beliefs and dreams. You do this without realizing it when you write a letter, have a conversation, attend a meeting, or conduct any other type of communication. There are no limits to networking—you are the center and can experience a life of greatness. Make networking the focus of your life and business. Think day and night about networking and you will see a miracle happen. There will be greatness in your life!

How often do you reflect upon the way you are living and the direction you are headed? Define, here, your method of assessing yourself. Specify the time frame and the items you wish to consider.

I will assess my progress every (frequency) _____

I will examine my (items) _____

_____

_____

In what way will reaching your goals make your life more satisfying?

_____

_____

_____

Do you see that what you are doing now is an important stepping stone to what you will be doing five years from now? Are you ready to make changes in your life? Scientists tell us that every seven years all the cells in the body make at least one complete change. A "new you" every seven years! Let's help mother nature by making it a successful you!

GETTING TO THE TOP FAST

True knowledge of yourself is probably the most difficult challenge you will ever face. At this point, hopefully you have already adopted or are already using several of the success techniques and skills that are presented here. But I realize that making changes in your method of doing things is a difficult process, isn't it?

Change usually begins when your current approach to the top isn't getting you there. The knowledge that our life or career strategy is not working usually approaches us gradually. Sometimes the drudgery of the grind clouds the realization that we're not getting anywhere. We may feel vaguely dissatisfied without knowing why. We don't get much fun out of what we're doing, and we can't see clearly where we're going. There is often a feeling that we may be wearing the rut so deeply that one day we will be unable to see over the sides. If you feel this way, you are ready for a change! Take a minute and assess whether you are on the road to prosperity, or whether you are running on the hamster's wheel.

RESISTANCE TO CHANGE

Homeostasis is the tendency to cling to the status quo. Avoiding change is a common human trait. Unfortunately, it is also a self-defeating and self-destructive habit. In reality life is change. We become accustomed to situations in everyday life such as dead-end jobs, professions we dislike, unsuccessful relationships, and other conditions that make our lives miserable. Even at an early age we are acutely aware of our own resistance to change. I've concluded that the heart of the problem is fear—fear of the unknown. To overcome such fear, the first thing you must do is face the reality that circumstances surrounding your life will change regardless of whether you want them to. The major unknowns will be how and when. It's up to you to decide whether you want to direct the changes, or whether you're content to react to them. The choice of directing the changes or just reacting to them will determine the control you have in your life.

So you have a problem? That's good, because every time you meet a problem and tackle it by making changes, you become a more successful person—a doer. Your success or failure in meeting these problems will be determined by your mental attitude.

Why not assign a positive attribute to the challenge rather than a negative one? If you think of change as the essence of life, as an exciting, integral part of the living experience, you can wipe fear from your consciousness. This can be easy, as I have found that change is exciting. I never cease to be amazed when I look back on my life and see how many major changes have taken place in a relatively short time, and how most of them have been for the better. At this point you have to prepare yourself for the change and review your strategy.

Here are a few suggestions for doing things differently by making new goals to find better ways of replacing losing habits with winning actions:

1. Change your daily schedule. Look over your daily routine. Are you doing the same things at the same time, day after day? If you alter your routine, you may look at every task from a different perspective. This gives you the opportunity to place more demanding, creative tasks earlier in the day while you are at your freshest. You may defer the more mundane tasks toward the end of the day. By having more discretionary time, you may decide upon working out a good strategy to tackle the project of reordering your life.

2. Do something doable. Pick up something you're sure you can do and do it. It doesn't have to be something big. Accomplishing something that is within your scope can give you a lift and get you eager for more ambitious undertakings tomorrow. As an example, start with doable mechanical tasks such as sorting, cleaning, straightening, routine mailing, paying bills, or some other easy project. You'll find yourself enjoying a small but distinct feeling of accomplishment. You'll be more ready to go about the job of improving your strategy in a positive frame of mind.

3. Form new habits of success. In devising a winning strategy, select effective tactics and decide to make them habits that will help you get closer to what you want. The schematic pattern of a habit starts with feeling a need. We take an action that satisfies

the need. We feel a reward, so when we feel the need we repeat the action that makes it become a habit.

The best way to get rid of bad habits is to replace them. We can acquire a good habit the same way that bad habits are acquired, as a recurring satisfying response to a need. A combination of common sense and trial and error is usually the method of determining a substitute. The new habit fills the need and makes you feel in control of yourself. Whenever you want to change a habit, convince yourself of the benefits of the new approach. Reinforcement is needed at a conscious level as well as an unconscious level. Observe and write down what the new action accomplishes. Next, provide yourself with rewards for success and penalties for failure. Strictly establish the responses to your actions and stick to them. For example, if you are trying to make a habit of getting your most difficult tasks accomplished in the morning, reward your success by going to a movie or other event. This approach is a good start to doing things differently and finding better ways of achieving goals. You can start replacing losing habits with winning actions.

The following are some questions you should answer on how you can manage the transition from a strategy that's getting you nowhere to one that will take you where you want to go:

What changes would you like to make in your life?

_____

_____

_____

_____

_____

What steps will you take to make these changes?

_____

_____

_____

_____

_____

When will these steps be taken?

_____

_____

_____

_____

_____

☑ BOE'S GUIDE #7: If you want something to happen, make it happen. It's foolhardy to sit back and wait for things to happen. The wise person cultivates the habit of making things happen. Many people naively assume that everyone else is vitally interested in their affairs. Particularly, it is important to realize that no one cares about what is important to you as much as you do. Perhaps you've had the experience that if someone wants something from you, your phone will ring off the hook. When you need cooperation from someone else, you can't seem to find anyone to help you. The point is, if you have something important to do, don't wait for others to take action. You deserve to have your dreams come true.

Making things happen takes a positive attitude and a resolve to take action. To take the first steps, you must prepare physically and mentally. Later you will see how to put your "self" in the proper frame of mind.

A NETWORKING FIRST

A colleague of mine and fellow networker, Diane O'Brien, shared with me her first encounter with networking. Diane has a direct mail advertising business and conducts seminars in direct mail and how to start your own successful business. This is her story:

Approximately twelve years have passed since a dear friend invited me to my first breakfast networking meeting. Not knowing what to expect, I hesitantly walked into a room of at least twenty other networkers. I was warmly greeted by a welcoming committee. As I went to get a cup of coffee and serve myself at the buffet, looking for a corner to hide in, I noticed that several people were expressing "host" type behaviors and exchanging friendly greetings. At first I panicked, thinking that I only knew one person in the room! I would have to talk to strangers! I was thankful that we were wearing name tags—afraid I'd forget someone's name.

I was witnessing others easily and gracefully building their net of connections, giving without expectations, sharing resources and information with each other. Soon I felt comfortable after getting considerable practice by answering the question, "What type of business are you in?" At this point, I thought it sure would be great to have a thirty-second commercial mentally prepared. I "winged" it, getting better with practice. It didn't take long before I felt more at ease. I genuinely became fascinated in other networkers' professions or businesses. Several people I met at this first networking meeting are still friends or business acquaintances.

I realized that everyone in the room could have had the same experience of wondering what to say, perhaps feeling ill at ease, uncomfortable or isolated. They didn't; they seemed to genuinely appreciate the opportunity to communicate. As my friend said to me, "Just show up and do it!" So, I took a deep breath and dove in. As I circulated around the room to meet others, I came across a large table that had brochures, business cards and displays of products and services that other networkers were offering. I realized that this was a very effective method of not only selling, but telling. I took one of each for future reference.

Little did I know the best was yet to come—the guest speaker. And, wonders of wonders, that speaker was Anne Boe to speak about the topic of networking! Imagine my first network meeting and getting coaching from the best! Well, from that meeting on, I've been hooked on networking. Anne's techniques and skills always stayed prominently on my mind. Even today, I can still vividly visualize her enthusiasm toward networking. I particularly enjoyed her positive attitude toward life, and fun. I saw from her example that networking did have a "fun" element while incorporating professional and personal accomplishments. I left with the faith and courage to practice networking to better my personal life and career.

After I left that meeting, I recapped all that went on. I had already inquired about information regarding membership, dues, and how (if I made the commitment to join) I could contribute to the network. In my hands was an unbelievable collection of business cards. Thanks to Anne's recommendation I wrote notes on the back of the cards that would help identify the people I met. Some of those notes included: the meeting place, the contact's work description, appearance, and any other interesting notes about our meeting. Next, I filed the cards according to type of business rather than by name. My first network meeting and among a large amount of networking information was great advice from Anne on what to do with all those business cards! Today I still have and use many of those cards.

I'm glad I attended the breakfast and glad I approached networking with an open mind. Networking has helped me achieve and obtain more contacts, given me more ideas and a bigger frame of reference with more exposure. I know that to get fast results, I must let others know what I want and what I need. This all happened when I started giving as much as I could, and ended up receiving much more. Yet I'm always impressed when someone goes out of their way for me. A networker has a way of living, not just as an individual, but also as a resource.

The exciting thing about networking is seeing the results for not only me but others. Now, I cannot imagine not networking. It allows me to work effectively to accomplish results with greater efficiency, ease, and satisfaction. It is a natural desire we have to serve and support one another, part of our heritage forever. I've learned to focus on it, organize it, and become sophisticated about it. I no longer cringe when I hear the icebreaking question, "What do you do?" With ease I let others know who I am, what I do well, and what I am currently working on. In this way I can effectively approach people and let them know what I need. Leads sometimes have a way of forming their own greater accomplishments: sales, money, and results. Networking means having the opportunity of getting to know somebody.

NOW IT'S YOUR TURN

Everyone has a networking story to share. Define what networking means to you and how it has had a positive influence on your personal and professional life.

2
NETWORKING IS AN INSIDE JOB!

"If you feel it in your heart,
you will have it in your life!"

Networkers know how to connect their heart and head energies. They can listen from their heart and hear their desires, beliefs, dreams and values. In this chapter we will explore you. You'll discover what is important to you and what makes you happy. Networking is energy management the ability to know what you want and having the courage to take action. Knowing what you want leads to goals that allow you to thrive in the present and to increase your chances of achieving long-term happiness.

GOALS AND WHAT YOU WANT

For most, it takes more than daily survival to feel content. A person must have more—a meaning to life—a purpose. The term "meaning to life" can have a higher spiritual meaning, but also can be defined to mean career, occupational goal, and normal, day-to-day living.

As I review my life and other people's life experiences, I am convinced that striving towards goals is not the means to an end; striving is an end in itself. I highly recommend that you enjoy each day as you work toward your goal. Enjoy the trip as much as the destination. Learn to laugh at yourself. Angels fly because they take themselves lightly!

Creating goals can be like charting your life's journey. Once you reach or arrive at your destination (goal), take a little time to savor the moment and then move on to your next destination (goal). There will always be more goals to achieve, more deals to close, more hills to climb. That's why you have to enjoy the present—each day of the trip. An unknown author put it much more simply when he/she said, "Yesterday is a canceled check; tomorrow is a promissory note; but today is cash in hand!"

If you are ready to commit to the necessary time and effort, you will acquire significant knowledge and wisdom that will help you reach your personal and career goals.

YOUR PRESENT LIFE

You can't get where you want to go until you know where you're coming from. To make changes in your person and in your life-style, you have to know who you are today. Look within to answer the following questions:

Are you pleased with your use of your personal (nonworking) time? Describe your satisfaction in terms of fulfillment.

_____

_____

_____

_____

_____

Are you happy with your current job? Why or why not?

_____

_____

_____

_____

_____

How many hours per week do you spend at work? _____

How many hours do you have that are not accountable for work hours? _____

How do you spend your non-work hours each day?

_____

_____

_____

_____

Each week?

_____

_____

_____

_____

Each month?

_____

_____

_____

_____

Do you feel you are financially rewarded for your work efforts?

_____

_____

_____

_____

What are your career talents?

_____

_____

_____

_____

What are your greatest strengths?

_____

_____

_____

_____

Do you feel good about your daily activities? Why or why not?
What would you choose to change?

_____

_____

_____

_____

_____

AFFIRMATIONS ARE POWERFUL

An affirmation is a positive declaration of action, intent, or conviction, usually designed to make one aware of or improve upon one's good aspects. Often, just the statement of the affirmation, particularly when repeated daily, makes it so. In other words, the more you hear the affirmation, the more you are convinced of its truth. You will be surprised at how often the simple affirmation becomes fact. Use affirmations and comments in your daily life— many are presented in this book. You may want to say them aloud and copy them on 3x5 cards and carry them with you. Repeat them daily and observe the remarkable results.

AFFIRMATIONS SET CREATIONS INTO MOTION

Affirmations should be part of your creative process as you state your desires. When you create something you will have more deliberate control of your current life situation. State your desire, intend it to be, and then allow it to happen. By stating your desire, you are clearly defining to yourself and to the universe what it is that you want. By intending it to be, you are putting universal forces into action, both within you and within that which is around you. And then allow it to happen. Often, one puts up roadblocks to the last step, usually by introducing thoughts that make it seem as if one is unworthy of the fulfillment. **Allowing** is the **most important part** of this equation. Many of us have long lists of unfulfilled wants, and although there is always room for improvement in clarifying precisely what it is that you are wanting, you need to allow yourself to be the receipt of what you want. This three step effort (desiring, intending, and allowing) is the creative process that we all have within us. Deliberate creating will result in much more joy and culmination in your life.

Remember, affirmations can be quite powerful, so always avoid any negatives. As an example, consider the statement, "I want to be the vice president of my company, even though I don't have enough experience." You see, you have given birth to your new career advancement on the one hand, and in the same breath you have removed the possibility of receiving it by your statement that it is not within reach. That which you are trying to create is voided in just that way.

The statement, "I want be president of my own company" should be enough of an affirmation. Better yet, say "I intend to be the President of my own company!" Offer only those thoughts and words that are in the direction of what you **truly** want. You are setting creation into motion through your thoughts, whether you understand that you are or not. Remember as you are stating that which you want, the more intense the emotion within you, and the more resolve to intend it to happen, the faster you will receive it.

AFFIRMATIONS

I know that I am surrounded by love and immersed in love.

My body is my home.

My body as it is now at its present size and in its present shape is an expression of divine love.

I allow myself to enjoy myself as I am knowing that I am surrounded by love and acknowledge my true nature.

I like being alive and being in love!

I love myself enough to allow myself to change.

I am perfect, whole and complete and know that my healthy body is in perfect working order.

I accept and let myself be myself.

My joy is welling up inside me and bubbling over the edges!

There is no struggle involved in my networking. I simply let go and let my heart be my guide.

I trust my intuition.

I am a fabulous loyal friend!

Everyone likes me!

I always expect to win!

I am a compassionate person who knows how to give and receive love, money, energy, and joy!

Create your own positive affirmations to suit your particular situations.

☑BOE'S GUIDE #8: Take care of yourself. Self-care is an art. Unless you have the courage to fall in love with yourself and to tell the truth to yourself, you will never be a true networker. Networking is a very compassionate and sensitive way of relating to other people. And the first person you must relate to is yourself. As a beginning to loving yourself, look at what others see when they see you—your body.

I LOVE MY BODY

You need to love your body and health as it is right now. It doesn't matter what shape your body is in—it is serving as a vehicle for life. Of course, it is a good idea to do whatever you can to keep your body at its best. Your body is a precious vessel of life force and energy. It doesn't matter whether you are experiencing a condition that we call illness, you can be thankful you are alive and praise and honor your body. Your body will respond to the direction you give it. If you say "I am fat" long enough your body will not lose weight and may even gain weight. If you continue to say, "I am limber, flexible, and strong," you will observe and feel greater mobility. Health needs to be one of your most important values and attributes.

SKILL BUILDER

Think of attributes that you genuinely like about your body and make a list. Say a few of those attributes out loud today.

What, if any, changes would you make to your body and/or health?

_____

_____

_____

_____

Be kind to yourself and protect your precious life energy. Learn to set boundaries, be there for yourself, and do loving things for yourself. As you nurture yourself, you will be more open to receiving. Support and love others. People want to give to you, so open your heart and feel that you are deserving, that you are special, and that you have a profound ability to love you and others. Networkers live by demonstration!

Make it a point not to say anything negative about your body or health for one week. If you slip, quickly correct yourself and replace the negative with a positive. Learn to praise and accept your body "as is," and identify areas where you want to improve. Write your goals for your ideal body weight and shape. Define your exercise, sport, and activity plans. See your inner and outer beauty. Networking energy comes from inside you. Some call it charisma—I call it being fully alive and aware of who you are and what you have to give. Set your time and schedule, and see yourself accomplishing your goals. Do so on the next page:

_____
_____
_____
_____
_____
_____
_____
_____
_____
_____
_____
_____

AFFIRMATIONS

My body is full of life, love, and perfect health.

I am complete, whole and beautiful.

I love and accept myself as I am.

My body is an expression of perfect life energy and nurturing.

I protect my precious life energy daily by listening to my body's signals.

MY ADDITIONAL AFFIRMATIONS

_____
_____
_____
_____
_____
_____
_____

☑ BOE'S GUIDE #9: Networkers have the courage to fall in love with themselves. Networking is a heartfelt activity that allows you to be the person you are meant to be and not the likeness of someone else's vision. It's amazing how many people follow somebody else's rules and somebody else's goals and somebody else's game plan! How many people do you know who are in relationships where they are not truly happy and they are not feeling value! Sometimes people need to be pushed to the brink before they realize that this life belongs to them, not to the demands and desires of others.

Try saying this out loud a few times: "I freely choose what I want, and what I choose to do, I can do." Feel the sense of release, of freedom, of unburdening? The first person you need to value is yourself. You need to look in the mirror and say to yourself, I am valuable because of these reasons:

ATTITUDE IS EVERYTHING

When you talk to others, everything about you and your business proclaims your attitude. Your attitude starts with knowing the importance of becoming happy with yourself. Perhaps, you have heard the saying, "You have to love yourself before you can love others." When you work from your heart and later connect your business sense, which is your head, you will be happy about your life. To have a positive attitude is very important. You need to clean up any past hurts, past relationships, and/or anything that is keeping you from being the magnificent person you should be. You will never make your dreams come true if you are carrying around excess baggage. Once you rid yourself of mental barriers, you have opened yourself up to the world of networking.

You cannot love anyone else until you have loved you. Until you love yourself, you will put up a barrier to your prosperity and net worth. Networkers take down walls and build bridges. First, take down your resistance to being cared for, nurtured, given to, and yes, happy! When you open up and decide that you are worth it, and when you come from kindness, you will be like a magnet to attract the right things and people; you have to stay within your goals, focus, and you need to follow the guides that are suggested in this book.

When you are with friends, do your interactions include much touching; for example, hugging and playfulness?

_____

_____

_____

Would you like to have more of this?

_____

_____

_____

How can you meet your relationship needs?

_____

_____

_____

_____

Define your desires for interaction with others.

_____

_____

_____

_____

YOUR BODY AND MIND WILL LET YOU KNOW

Your work should promote greater physical and emotional health. Your work can offer you the opportunity to advance, to enjoy a change in career, to connect deeply with people, to discover yourself, and to feel excitement. While all this sounds wonderful, there can be stress associated with these activities. By effectively learning to deal with changes from your heart, you will have a greater connection to your inner self and to other people.

Making changes can often lead to physical and mental stress. You will always be challenged to make changes and be faced with the decision whether changes will be worth the mental and/or physical price. It is human nature to gravitate toward a process that involves less pain and more pleasure. Often, less pain equates to laziness or procrastination. You must determine if your activities are in the direction of your goals, or if they are only deterring you from your goals. Sometimes, you must look ahead and realize that the results of your efforts will be to accomplish your goals. Then, the stress involved with the effort becomes less significant, therefore, less stressful. The "thrill of the desire" can easily overcome the "strain of the effort" if you develop a confident attitude. The chore can become a delightful affair.

A certain amount of stress can be good for you, giving you a challenge; but too much stress can give you emotional discomfort or even symptoms of physical illness. Be aware of what is going on with your body, your heart, and your mind because these areas are the residence of the power of networking. Your body is always talking to you. Listen to these inner messages. They are your love and health guides.

There is a principle associated with the law: "Actions have consequences: The higher the price, the greater the benefit." The good news is that when you develop the ability to correctly perceive the benefits, you will be able to deal effectively with changes that lead to having a sense of well being and inner peace.

☑ BOE'S GUIDE #10: Networkers are always true to themselves. Rid yourself of the fear of telling the truth about you. As you spend time with you and going within, you will get closer to your heart's desire. You may have to peel off layers from your facade. You may have to go through some pain and hurt knowing that the rewards will be tenfold. Know that you have the freedom to live the way you want to live. You can have the relationships that are loving and supportive, and you will be able to give as well as receive.

Networkers are leaders, not followers. To be a good leader, you must learn to follow from within, from your heart, and from your intuition as you listen and act upon your inner voice. You are the only one who knows what is best for you. One of my workshop sayings is, "No one has to tell you when it's right." Please learn to trust yourself and learn to use your inner voice as your inner guide and friend.

"Just trust yourself, then you will know how to live."
                                                              —Goethe

HEART OVER MIND DOES MATTER

Do you understand the difference between head and heart energies? Do you believe that there is a spirit within that is your driving force, and that often your conscious thoughts are out of tune from your inner spirit guidance mechanisms? The difference between acting from your mind compared to your heart within is that the mind deals only with memorized, subjective and objective experiments, while your inner self (the heart) extracts and employs the generalized principles that strive toward fulfillment of your purpose in life. The brain deals exclusively with the physical, while your inner guidance (the heart) combines the mind, body, and spirit.

HEARTFELT WORDS LEAD TO ACTION

One of the key points to remember is that action is best driven by desire, and desire comes from the heart. Many times you "know what you should do," but for whatever reason, you don't follow through. This can be analyzed by looking at the word, "know." This is a mind word, not a heart word. By rephrasing to "I feel that I will . . ." you can envision a much more likely probability that you will follow through. This is because you are letting your intuition and your feelings dictate your actions. Have you ever noticed a "gut feeling" about something, and after following through, felt as though you were glad you did? Conversely, have you not followed through and regretted it? These are examples of your inner guidance system that is much more in tune with your true self. Your brain is usually brainwashed by others from the time you were born. Your heart is your true self. List examples of times when you followed your intuition and had successful results personally and professionally:

_____   _____
_____
_____
_____
_____
_____

CONNECT YOUR HEART AND HEAD ENERGIES

The heartbeat of networking is your ability to care about people. Even if you learn all the skills, say all the right things and go through all the motions, networking will be effective only if genuine human caring exists. A primary goal of this guidebook is for you to discover the importance of "coming from the heart" by learning to connect your heart and your head energies and to always come from kindness and sincerity. Look for the good in everyone and that is what you will experience.

Anybody can be a good talker or a good listener, but often the words are just that—words that one is parroting (buzzwords) or words that one thinks will put a listener at ease (saying what another is wanting to hear). These words are not from the heart. You can be a great networker and a great career strategist if you communicate from the heart. The secret to business and life relationship success is to feel the emotion and the power of your heart energy.

HOW TO PUT YOUR HEAD IN YOUR HEART'S HANDS

Once you understand yourself you will draw from your power within. At every one of my speeches throughout corporate America, I always say, "Spend at least five minutes a day going within and listening to your heart." Success is not success unless you, the networker, feel good about what you are doing. That means staying in your integrity and in your value systems—following your heart! Can you imagine the power of networking from the heart and the benefits that networking can have on your career and personal life? Do the exercises in this book by expressing from your heart!

☑ BOE'S GUIDE #11: Networking is very empowering—whatever you give out, comes back. Everybody reading this book is going to have a chance to develop their most powerful mental and intuitive faculties. You may find yourself, during the course of this journey, getting frustrated at times and may feel like just giving in. If this should happen, may I make a suggestion? Go to the beach or the park! That's right! Going to the beach or the park provides an excellent opportunity to think clearly; to review one's life, to recall earlier frustrations, and to ponder abandoned longings, and curiosities. It is a fabulous place to meditate—to clean out the old and let in the new.

Networkers are not afraid of letting go. The art of surrendering is critical to the networkers' success. Whether you are at the beach or at work, what I want you to do is to think and feel clearly. By dealing with each challenge in our life we gradually uncover where we are at this time in our life. For us to progress to the future, we must be prepared for the present. We must know where we are, where we want to be, and what we must do to get there. Boe's Guides are designed for you to practice the steps that lead to self-confidence and conviction. Most importantly, they will help you gain a mastery of communication. This is the essence of what this book is about.

The secrets to good networking lie within you and depend on how you relate to yourself and the world around you. The key is to tap into your inner resources while wisely using your outer resources, your networking support system.

People who succeed in life are those who have welcomed the challenge that life gives them. They communicate that experience to themselves (listening from within) in a way that causes them to successfully change their environment toward that which they desire. Will you agree with me on that? I hope so, because the whole point of this book is that the knowledge, drive, and skills within you are the essence of what will make you happy and fulfilled. These qualities can be expanded and intensified if you are willing to invest time and effort and money into yourself. Is there any better investment than yourself?

SKILL BUILDER

How do you visualize networking as enhancing your business and career opportunities?

_____

_____

_____

_____

_____

ANSWER FROM YOUR HEART

When you are working with these lessons, be as honest as you can. There is a difference between changing your thinking and denying your feelings. There is no value in pretending to be somewhere or someone you are not. So tell today's truth. The only place to be during a journey is where you are now. The direction you should be going is toward the place where you want to be. Your work can be the most fascinating work you will ever do. You are embarking on a study of the grammar of your soul. The rewards for opening your heart will be astounding. You are coming home to you! Welcome back networkers!

EXPECT RESULTS!

It is wonderful to see instant results and I believe you will achieve many surprises very quickly if you apply what you learn to your life. After the initial thrill of success and easy small gains, you may not see the immediate rewards that you expected. Some issues take a longer time to work through, but eventually they can be eased or completely changed. Don't get discouraged. Our ego always wants to see its way clear before it acts. It prefers mental conflict now to simple actions. It would rather pause and stew than move easily forward, and so it uses its favorite delaying tactic: the question of right and wrong. In these cases a simple suggestion is needed, so rely on your inner guidance by asking what action will restore inner peace or calm in your life.

You have a right to a good and prosperous life. You have achieved the level of understanding that brought you into contact with this material. Your inner guidance system may have led you to pick up this book. Therefore, you are ready. You may have heard of the saying, "When the student is ready, the teacher appears." Approach it joyfully with an open heart. A beginning driver must learn the rules and meanings of safety signs before going out on the road. Likewise, a beginning or growing businessperson must learn some rules and guides as well.

YOUR FIRST "HEART" QUESTIONS

Does the fact that you have never done something before increase or decrease its appeal to you? Why or why not?

_____

_____

_____

_____

If you could wake up tomorrow morning having gained any one ability or quality, what would it be?

_____

_____

_____

Is happiness more important to you than wealth, or are they indistinguishable to you? Why?

_____

_____

_____

_____

☑ BOE'S GUIDE #12: Networkers know how to manage and focus their energy. Your energy is your life and your life consists of decisions you make every day. You only have so much precious life energy and you will often be faced with choices. The secret to networking that leads to net worth and success in the business world is being clear on your objectives, having a backup plan, and becoming your own career strategist. Mary, is an example of being clear on her objectives and having a backup plan. She became a care head at the Mercy Hospital in San Diego by working her way up from secretary to the president's assistant. When her employer left, Mary was asked to head the search committee to find his replacement. After nine months the committee couldn't find a replacement candidate. Mary took action by telling them that she knew more about the hospital than anyone, and she proposed herself as the ideal replacement. She insisted that she was best for the position. She was granted the position, and did a phenomenally successful tenure as president of Mercy Hospital.

Where did Mary and others like her get the confidence to take such bold action? First, they were all confident in their abilities due to a good track record. Equally important, they get support and validation from other people. Of course, they have high expectations that help build self-confidence.

POWER IN THE FORCES

Many of us realize that we want inner power. Power can be enormously challenging and fun. While you are working hard, make certain you are working in the right direction. Too many people think that unrestrained hard work is the secret of success.

Unfortunately, this type of virtue isn't always rewarded in the business world. To get to the top, you have to understand your company's power route. Then you must determine if you are on the right road or going up a blind alley.

Power just doesn't fall into your lap. Happily-ever-after endings occur only in fairy tales and old Horatio Alger novels. These are times that try our soul and build vision. We must become much stronger and resilient, waiting until we get what we want. Furthermore, we must stay united, for in unity there is strength. Never underestimate the power of any collective force, and don't underestimate the weakness of a house divided. Today is not the time to fight and compete—it is the time to cooperate. If we all pull together, never again will anyone ever underestimate the power of networkers. Remember:

- Don't be afraid of success; it's much more fun than failure.
- The sky's the limit; raise your expectation level.
- Believe in yourself, and everyone else will, too.
- Confidence is contagious.
- Networking is fun and profitable!

☑ BOE'S GUIDE #13: Networkers believe they deserve the best. Part of achieving career, financial, and relationship success through networking is believing in yourself. You create your own reality through your thoughts. If you are always putting yourself down, and always thinking about what non-positive things happened to you at three, six, or ten years old, then you are robbing yourself of a positive attitude. One of my favorite quotes is: "Time is a dressmaker specializing in alterations." As we go through change in this economy and as we work to learn to use change as a challenge and growth opportunity to stay ahead of the competition, it is very important that you feel good about you.

CREATIVE VISUALIZATION: A STEP BEYOND

Another step to get what you want in life is creating to see the future as you want it to be. See the fulfillment of your goal or see it as far as you can see it through. See yourself arriving at whatever destination or point of achievement. Envision yourself taking the step to get where you want to be and feel the emotion. You see, when you understand the power that your emotion and desire brings, then you will be faster at creating that which you want. Contentment comes from allowing and then receiving. You want it, you allow it, you receive it; and the contentment comes from the process. Your payment due is a sincere thank you!

"The imagination may be compared to Adam's dream—
he awoke and found it truth."

—Keats

SKILL BUILDER
How do you visualize?

_____
_____
_____
_____
_____
_____

What senses do you use?

_____
_____
_____
_____
_____

What's it like?

_____
_____
_____
_____
_____

It's easy to visualize. Think of the pyramids in Egypt. Now think of the Statue of Liberty. Now think of a lemon. Next think of a rose. What color is the rose? If it's red, make it yellow; if it's yellow make it red. Think of a waterfall. Think of the ocean on a clear, sunny day. How do you feel? These are all examples of visualizing.

EVERY THOUGHT HAS CREATIVE POWER

One of the first things to understand is that you are constantly directing and attracting **creative energy** to provide new experiences in your life. The thoughts that you think set into motion the creation and eventual fulfillment of those things that you want. Also, the thoughts that you think regarding those things that you do not want set into motion the creation and eventual fulfillment of that which you do not want. You create through your thoughts.

As you look at your life experience, you may immediately recognize that what you have experienced, and are experiencing, is in reality what you have drawn into your life through your thought. Be careful of what you think or wish for because thoughts and wishes do come true! They may not show up exactly as you imagined and planned for, but they will be realized.

SKILL BUILDER

Can you think of times when you had experiences of getting what you wanted? Please list some.

_____

_____

_____

_____

☑ BOE'S GUIDE #14: Networkers know never to hurt themselves or anyone else. Sometimes, the best feelings are those that you have when you are giving. Conversely, when you are in a position to share and don't, your feeling of satisfaction is very limited. Anytime you cause pain to another through your actions or inaction, you are guaranteeing yourself a less rewarding experience. The whole concept of hurt—regardless of the physical, emotional, or mental aspect—is a form of negative energy. As you should know by now, all things negative should be avoided.

KNOWLEDGE LEADS TO WISDOM AND POWER

As you participate in this book, you will encounter decision opportunities to make changes in your life. The ideas expressed in the book will give you knowledge, and the daily practice of the ideas will give you wisdom. Knowledge can be gained through reading and understanding how it works. Wisdom, however, is even more important than knowledge in that it involves common sense, good judgment, and total comprehension. Knowledge is the awareness of the subject matter; whereas, wisdom is the experience of knowledge. A knowing person can tell you the facts. A wise person can give you insight as to how the facts work within the scheme of things. Knowledge is in the physical and is mind associated. Wisdom is universal, spiritually associated, and leads to inner peace, fulfillment, and self-empowerment.

"It is not enough to have a good mind.
The main thing is to use it well."
              —RENE DESCARTES, 1637

EXERCISE
Write one of your life's experiences depicting how knowledge can lead to wisdom.

_____

_____

_____

_____

_____

_____

_____

_____

_____

_____

AFFIRMATIONS
I AM WHO I AM

I am the director of the positive energy flowing through my mind. My words and thoughts and emotions form that infinite energy into the conditions and circumstances of my life and environment.

"KNOWING YOURSELF" EXERCISES

Before you answer the following questions, give each considerable thought, and then set specific goals. Otherwise, you may one day realize that you wasted many years of your life trying to achieve goals that were not in harmony with who you really are. Answer the following questions:

1. What makes you happy?

_____

_____

_____

_____

_____

2. What are your most significant values?

_____

_____

_____

_____

_____

3. What is one of the best relationships you have in your life right now? What qualities make it so special?

_____

_____

_____

_____

_____

READER/CUSTOMER CARE SURVEY

If you are enjoying this book, please help us serve you better and meet your changing needs by taking a few minutes to complete this survey. Please fold it & drop it in the mail.

As a thank you, we will send you a gift.

Name: _____

Address: _____

_____

Tel. # _____

Gender: ____ Female ____ Male

Age: ____ 18-25   ____ 46-55
     ____ 26-35   ____ 56-65
     ____ 36-45   ____ 65+

Marital Status: ____ Married ____ Single
     ____ Divorced ____ Partner

Is this book: ____ Purchased for self?
     ____ Purchased for others?
     ____ Received as gift?

How did you find out about this book?

____ Catalog
____ Store Display
Newspaper
     ____ Best Seller List
     ____ Article/Book Review
     ____ Advertisement
Magazine
     ____ Feature Article
     ____ Book Review
     ____ Advertisement
____ Word of Mouth
____ T.V./Talk Show (Specify) _____
____ Radio/Talk Show (Specify) _____
____ Professional Referral _____
____ Other (Specify) _____

What subject areas do you enjoy reading most? (Rank in order of enjoyment)

____ Women's Issues   ____ New Age
____ Business Self Help   ____ Aging
____ Relationships   ____ Altern. Healing
____ Inspiration   ____ Parenting
____ Soul/Spirituality   ____ Diet/Nutrition
____ Recovery   ____ Exercise/Health
____ Other (Specify) _____

What do you look for when choosing a personal growth book? (Rank in order of importance)

____ Subject   ____ Author
____ Title   ____ Price
____ Cover Design   ____ In Store Location
____ Other (Specify) _____

When do you buy books? (Rank in order of importance)

____ Xmas   ____ Father's Day
____ Valentines Day   ____ Summer Reading
____ Birthday   ____ Thanksgiving
____ Mother's Day
____ Other (Specify) _____

Where do you buy your books? (Rank in order of frequency of purchases)

____ Bookstore   ____ Book Club
____ Price Club   ____ Mail Order
____ Department Store   ____ T.V. Shopping
____ Supermarket   ____ Airport
____ Health Food Store   ____ Drug Store
____ Gift Store   ____ Other (Specify)

Additional comments you would like to make to help us serve you better.

_____

_____

_____

Thank You !!

4. What adds joy to your life?

_____

_____

_____

_____

5. What gives you your greatest sense of energy?

_____

_____

_____

_____

6. What, until now, has been your greatest accomplishment, either personally or in your career?

_____

_____

_____

_____

7. What is it in your life that you still have not done and have a great desire to do?

_____

_____

_____

_____

8. What do you love most about you?

_____

_____

_____

_____

As you learn the art of self-care and self-nurturing, you will become happier, more congruent with your communication skills, and achieve more loving relationships. You will be like a magnet that attracts positive people, experiences, and events to you with less effort.

WARNING: THIS IS NOT A QUICK AND EASY EXERCISE—IT MAY TAKE THE REST OF YOUR LIFE TO ACCOMPLISH!

Spend some time imagining yourself having whatever you desire. You can, you know! If you were to choose one thing that would be first on your list of desires, what would it be? On the following worksheet make a list of everything you want to have, do, or be. The sky is the limit! Write down all your desires, goals, wants and needs. Include material, mental, emotional, physical, and spiritual goals. Then prioritize the list in order of importance on the following lines:

1. _____

2. _____

3. _____

4. _____

5. _____

6. _____

7. _____

8. _____

9. _____

10. _____

How do feel about writing and describing what you want? Most people find it difficult to truly know and prioritize what they would like to have in their life. Having a list helps us sort the opportunities that come our way. Writing it down helps us have a sense of direction to set realistic, achievable goals. Writing the goals down forces us to see them through, for if the ideas are not written, they could easily be forgotten. When staring back at us, those words are constantly reminding us to "go for it!" Also, this technique can help you answer the question that many of us avoid, "What am I going to do the rest of my life to bring in joy, career success, loving relationships, and a feeling of inner peace?"

With the above skill builder, avoid making excuses such as, if I only had more money, better health, more time, was prettier, younger, had better friends, or any other reasons for not having something. The reason for avoiding excuses is because if you did have more money, better health, more time, or whatever, you would soon want other things. For this exercise assume you have everything you need to make it possible to have whatever you want in your life. Finally, review your list and ask yourself the following questions:

How many things do I really want?

_____

_____

_____

Am I willing to make a plan and do the work required?

_____

_____

_____

Does having these things in my life lead to my true purpose?

_____

_____

_____

If you answer "no" to any of these questions, you will need to cross out and add replacements of what you would really like to have, do, or be, and what price you are willing to pay to get what you say you want. Commitment begins with you being willing to do whatever it takes to achieve your goals. Remember, networkers never hurt themselves or anyone else. Compassion and sensitivity remain at the top of a networker's priorities with self and with others.

OPENING YOUR HEART

How do you feel after experiencing the affirmations, comments and exercises? Are you able to comfortably open your heart? Most of us are not used to expressing feeling in writing, and some may find that they haven't done so here. It takes a brave person to open their heart. Remember, an open heart can't break because feelings felt are not as fragile as feelings not expressed. Expressing your feelings is a good way of releasing the stress of holding them in your heart.

Did you have any negative feelings? If so, feel those feelings and then let them go. We have a wonderful protective mechanism that occurs in the human body. We won't open our hearts until there is the capacity to handle what is there for us. Do you build a brick wall around your heart? You are strong—knock down each brick one by one. When that wall is knocked down, you will feel the magnificent nourishment of the sunshine and fresh air! Networkers break through walls and build bridges! Why not start now? You are worth it!

Quickly write down six beliefs that may be keeping you from opening your heart.

1. _____

2. _____

3. _____

4. _____

5. _____

6. _____

Be aware of the beliefs that keep your heart closed for protection. Remember, you have a right to protect yourself. Now, you are aware of what is closing your heart and you can begin to heal each negative belief. An open heart is a healthy happy heart where true networking relationships blossom and grow.

AFFIRMATIONS

I love myself and my heart is open as I radiate love and acceptance.

I am in tune with myself psychologically, physically and spiritually.

I am fully living my life with joy now.

I am present and emotionally available now.

Although there are no shortcuts or magic formulas, trust this book to be your guide for mastering knowledge, wisdom, techniques, and principles. You will discover nuggets of pure gold, waiting only for you to reach out and claim them as your own. Please remember, you need not accept or attempt to use all the success ideas and techniques you are learning. Just one may be all you need to work wonders in your life and career. All that is required of you is a burning desire to make something more of your life. The only limits are those that you place on yourself. You can master the skills of networking—it can be learned regardless of your age, your skills, your background, your ethnicity, your financial condition, or your opinion about yourself.

LEARNING TO TRUST YOURSELF

Are you ready to learn to trust yourself? Are you ready to stop passing the buck for your life and assume control? Are you ready to stop making excuses and start making progress? Are you ready to allow negative comments to roll off you like water off a duck? It's time to start trusting yourself—TODAY!

Once you decide to stop being dependent on other's feelings about you, to take charge, to be a master of your own destiny, you will begin to notice a new power and energy come into to your life. It may not happen instantly, but you'll begin to notice a new spirit overtake you. You will be more creative, happier, and confident, more at peace. Instead of a quiet desperation, you will exude a quiet power. Try it, you'll like it.

"GO FOR IT" GOALS

It amazes me why something as tiny as a thought can have such a dramatic effect on your mind, body, and emotions. Even the creation of human beings starts as a thought. As the old saying goes, "I knew you before you were a twinkling in your father's eye." Hopefully, through the exercises, your thoughts have helped you to know what you want. You may be wondering what are your next steps. If you answered, plan and action, you are absolutely correct. The process is:

- Thought - *the initial desire from the heart*
- Idea - *putting the thought into form*
- Goal - *defining the result you wish to achieve*
- Plan - *the method to see it through*
- Action - *"going for it"*
- Achievement and results - *the success of your efforts*

The following are a few ideas to help you turn your thoughts to successful action:

1. Parse each goal into achievable action steps. Some goals seem so large that they are overwhelming; but if split into several smaller portions, each new "sub-goal" seems more easily attainable. By accomplishing each portion, the larger goal eventually is accomplished by default. Have a passion about what you want and then be ready to take the necessary action. For example, if you want to change your career and know that you will need a degree to make this goal possible, you will make

decisions upon what college to attend, what courses to take, and other items relating to the degree requirement of your overall career goal. Once you start the process, be flexible and the next steps seem to naturally present themselves.

2. Plan your plan. When you see your goals in writing they seem more real. Your next step involves the action of taking out your calendar, daily planner, appointment book, or whatever you use to schedule your activities and start scheduling what you need to do to accomplish your goals. It's easy to procrastinate if you know there's no deadline. By planning your time, you also give yourself self-imposed milestones, and you also will find it easier to follow through with the plan than to make up excuses to avoid action. After all, since you are being true to your heart, you will know that the excuse is just that—it's not a valid reason.

Take time out, to analyze how you feel about taking the action. Are you feeling fear, boredom, resistance, or any other negative feelings? Whenever you make changes, expect these strong, controlling feelings. Many times these feelings may be saying, "I am trying to protect you," or "take the easy way." You should expect challenges along the way. Don't let these feelings stop you—you know what you need to do. Thank these feelings for their advice, let them go and move ahead.

3. Tap into your network. Know what you need and find the people who may help. Successful people understand the power of networking. Don't feel guilty about having someone open a door for you or offer insight into similar experiences. Once you get to where you want to be, there is the possibility that you will be able to extend a helping hand to someone else. Now is the time to examine your network and determine who can advise and assist you.

4. Be gentle on yourself and others. Don't be so possessed with your goal that you miss out on enjoying the process of getting there. Be kind, gentle and enjoy the journey. The only limits that prevent us from making our life's dreams a reality are the limits we put on ourselves.

5. Make your goal stronger than your fears. Fear is a part of your life. Feel it, accept it, and go through your own limitations and barriers. Ask yourself how badly you want your goal and if you are willing to take fear on. Take your butterflies and fly them in formation! Allow fear to work for you as you go towards what you want and deserve. The only person who can stop you is you! Ask someone in your network to help you get through your fear. Joy awaits you!

Will Rogers, bless his great heart, said:

Know what you are doing.
Love what you are doing.
Believe in what you are doing.

THE FUTURE

As you answer the following questions, ask yourself the price to reach these goals and if it is really worth it. Are you willing to pay the price? When considering what you want out of life, you have to give serious consideration to the cost. Although we may not know exactly what the cost is until we confront a situation, we realize that the cost can present itself in many forms, such as time, energy, pain, or sacrifice.

If you had to choose one personal goal to accomplish within one year, what would it be?

_____

_____

_____

If you had to choose one career goal to come into being within one year, what would it be?

_____

_____

_____

Why do you want the goal? In other words, what's in it for you?

personal: _____

_____

_____

career: _____

_____

_____

Write down two action steps that you can complete with your current resources and time within the next week that will start leading you toward your goal. As soon as you complete your action steps, please write down two more and do the same process again.

1. _____

_____

2. _____

_____

Goal setting is a very important process for a networker. Clarity is power and the clearer you are about your heart's desire, the easier it will be for you to draw in the right resources, information, advice, and energy.

Take a few minutes now to close your eyes and imagine that I am giving you a magic wand that has unlimited potential for power, resources, money, or whatever else you can imagine. You now have everything you need to accomplish what you want.

What would you most desire to do and/or to be, at this moment?

_____

_____

_____

_____

How does this differ from your current life or career situation?

_____

_____

_____

_____

What can you do to start bridging the gap between what you have
and what you truly desire from your heart?

_____

_____

_____

_____

Networkers know that inner joy creates inner peace that, in
turn, creates better health and more fulfilling relationships. It's
impossible to relate to someone else if you have all your energy
centered on you. Get out of your own way and live a little! You
may even have some fun!

PRACTICE IS YOUR KEY TO SUCCESS

Practice, practice, practice! That will be your key to success.
To quote Bobby Ross, the head coach of the San Diego Chargers,
"Practice doesn't make perfect—perfect practice makes perfect."
With networking, every little bit helps. So don't worry about what
might go wrong if you don't do something properly. Rather, delve
into the networking frame of mind at every opportunity. Create
your opportunities, and practice some more. Most people are willing
to read and grasp the surface of new ideas but only a few are
willing to put the time and energy into the necessary practice.

If you are trying to reach for the new, and feel as though you
are being grabbed and dragged back, realize who is putting up the
obstacle. It is your mind not wanting you to express or experience
something that is new, for it is seeking the comfort of sameness and
knowingness. This is true, for the most part, because your mind

does not understand the creative process. Now you are reawakened. You must trust your heart and try new experiences. You will always be growing, and wherever you are, you are just beginning.

PSYCHE UP!

The single-most important advantage that can be gained from networking is that you can be as successful as you'd like to be. There are no limits to the number of rewarding experiences you can receive from meeting others. Networking is variety. To a networker every day is an adventure. Every morning tell yourself that networking is challenging, exciting and fun. Look forward to it. Tell yourself that you can hardly wait to get started. Mean it! Psyche yourself up to enjoy the adventure. Then go for it! Look for and welcome networking opportunities. If you aspire to greatness, you will yearn to take down the wall and start building bridges. Everything begins with you and your attitude. Allow your positive attitude to work for you.

Personal Notes

3
A COMMUNITY OF COMMUNICATION

*"It takes two people to communicate
and both must be completely involved"*

Networking is the ability to relate and communicate to other people in any situation. This sounds like a simple statement until you realize that most people are not accustomed to expressing their feelings with strangers. Attending a gathering with strangers is the number one social fear, according to a study on "Social Anxiety," reported in the *New York Times* (December 18, 1984). Most people would rather speak in public (number two social fear) than attend an event where they would be meeting strangers. Therefore, you can assume that when you are uncomfortable while attending a networking event that you are not alone.

Like it or not, you have to deal with others to achieve any reasonable degree of success. This is true at all life stages. It stands to reason that the more successful you are in getting others to cooperate with you, and the more people you can solicit as allies, the greater your chances of achieving positive results. No more being the lone ranger! Networking is getting together to get ahead!

Good relationships begin with you. An individual can be brilliant at may things, yet be totally ineffective when it comes to getting along with, and gaining the cooperation of peers. Good communication skills can be learned. Anyone can become better at whatever they do through practice and having a caring attitude.

CREATING RELATIONSHIP MAGIC

Networkers know that everything in life is a relationship. Why do you go back to certain stores? Isn't it because a person perhaps recognized you, or was courteous to you, and in some way, relates to you? Having a relationship does not mean you're going to fall in love with everyone and does not mean that everyone becomes your best friend. It means that you are able to peacefully coexist and are able to provide a sense of comfort and benefit to each other.

Your network is only as powerful as your relationships. It enhances your ability to relate to others. You need to express interest and respond to the needs of people in your network. Look for opportunities to develop new friendships. Use expressions like "I'm looking for" or "I need" or "I want" and you'll find that other's are willing to help because it makes them feel needed and wanted. Have your business card available to hand to them. When conversing, tell them that they can use your name as a reference and they will surely take care of you then or in the future. Give more than you receive and you will get more than you need. Constantly ask what other people are doing and find out how you can support them. In return, they will support you and help you get what do you need. These types of relationships, your network of friends, become your **safety net**—the people you can always fall back on when you need them. Remember that this works both ways. There will always be times when they need you, and you will be very happy to be counted on and very happy to help.

Write some examples from your experience:

Lifelong supportive relationships: _____

_____

_____

_____

Needing support: _____

_____

_____

_____

Finding someone needing your support: _____

_____

_____

_____

A fulfilling feeling of accomplishment: _____

_____

_____

_____

The empowering part of networking is that you select your friends. You are in charge of your network and your feelings, and you are the one who can control your destiny. Keep developing the ability to take advantage of the opportunities to get outside yourself long enough to show interest in someone else. Add value to every person you meet and watch the magic begin! Friendships are built on loyalty and commitment. They are developed through meticulous attention to people, a true concern for others, and a genuine caring for another. In other words, nurture your network daily!

Networkers move through a room with ease and grace. We want to feel comfortable no matter what the type of event: a party, meeting, convention, fund-raiser, cocktail event, reunion, political gathering, or social evening. No matter what the setting, you must genuinely care about the people you interact with to be successful at networking. Your warmth, your openness, and your desire to connect with other networkers must be honest and sincere.

Enjoy cocktail talk. Ask the person you are talking to whether they have been at this function or meeting before. You may also ask them a specific question about their work. You may say something like, "I bet you really enjoyed that! It appears that you really do a good job with your customer base!" It takes attention, listening, and sincerity on your part.

The best approach is to have fun. Others will be interested in you because they will see your self-confidence and your enjoyment of communicating with them. The good news is that you will have a good time while other personal and professional benefits follow.

SKILL BUILDER

Since so many individuals place great emphasis on a happy personal life, why do people often wind up putting more energy into their professional lives?

_____

_____

_____

If you feel your personal life is more important to you, are your priorities aligned appropriately?

_____

_____

Are you simply unwilling to admit that work is more important?

_____

_____

Do you use work as a substitute?

_____

_____

_____

Do you hope professional success will somehow magically lead to personal happiness?

_____

_____

What makes you happy?

_____

_____

_____

_____

What would you like to correct to add more joy to your life?

_____

_____

_____

_____

What is most important to you now, personally?

_____

_____

_____

_____

What is most important to you now, professionally?

_____

_____

_____

_____

Life is really simple! What we give out we get back. Enjoy today!

☑ BOE'S GUIDE #15: Networkers always expect to win. I am always shocked when I do not get hired for a keynote speaking engagement. My secretary always says, "Anne, you cannot have everything!" We both laugh when I always answer, "Yes I can and I expect it!" I am astonished when I do not get what I want whereas most non-networkers are surprised when they do. I want you to always expect to win. To do this, you may need to change your belief systems. If you want to know what your belief systems are, look at the results you are currently experiencing in your life. Your outer world is a direct reflection of your inner thoughts. The simplicity and the beauty of networking is this: if you want to change your outer world and become more prosperous, then you need to start with your inner belief systems. Write down a few of your current beliefs.

After you have filled in these beliefs, analyze what you have written and ask yourself if the beliefs are working toward your networking success. Do they come from your heart, or are they the by-product of what some others in your life have told you to believe? Are there any beliefs listed that could be sabotaging your business success? Are there any beliefs that, in any way, say to you that you do not believe in yourself? If you see any that are not in synchronization with where you want to be, then tell yourself that the belief is no longer to be a part of your being. Go back and cross out the contrary belief, and know in your heart that you will no longer have any part of it!

FALLING IN LOVE WITH YOURSELF

At each of my motivational keynote speeches, I always say, "Take the time to fall in love with yourself and give yourself the courage to change." People would rather be comfortable than change. If you keep doing exactly what you're doing, you will get the same results. Congratulations if you're happy, healthy, prosperous, and full of every joy that you ever wanted. Most people aren't—that's why they turn to networking.

AFFIRMATIONS

I am my best friend.

I will take care of myself.

I love myself unconditionally.

I will continue to learn and grow.

I will develop and share my love and life.

☑ BOE'S GUIDE #16: Networkers know that the saddest words in the English language are "I wish I would have." Networkers, the past is over. Never do I want you to say "I wish I would have." People rarely regret the big things—they tend to regret the little things. They regret the time they were at a meeting or function and they didn't cross a room and say to someone, "I think your an interesting person and I'd like to talk to you." They regret the time they didn't say "Thank-you," or the time they didn't say "I love you," or the time they didn't say "I would like to work with you," or the time they didn't say "I really want to get to know you." Networkers take the time to do these things on a regular basis. No regrets—only new goals.

ALL SUCCESSFUL PEOPLE "LIVE" NETWORKING

Networkers live in the moment. You have compassion, but you know that this is not a dress rehearsal. You can't go back! Do it now! Networkers go after opportunities while they build lasting relationships. They create friendships that last and that bring them inner joy and happiness. The greatest joy you can have is connecting your heart and your head energies so you become the magnificent, successful, prosperous person that you are meant to be. Have the courage to be you—there is no one as special as you!

At least three times a week, call a person that you haven't seen in a long time. Make a note to yourself of what you talked about, and schedule a "tickler" to yourself to follow with another call soon. Pick up the next conversation exactly where you left off, showing the other person that you are interested in the topic and in the other person's thoughts and opinions. Your attention will be respected and appreciated. Mutual giving and receiving of trust and respect will keep your network alive and prosperous.

☑ BOE'S GUIDE #17: Networking is a very compassionate process. You earn the right to have a friend and you earn the right to do business with someone. You also earn the right to lose a friendship or be shunned by others. It is important to realize how these two outcomes result—they are a direct result of your efforts and your sincerity. Do not treat your relationships in a flippant manner. Be more concerned with relationships than with end results. Be compassionate and caring. Here are some steps to building and nurturing successful relationships.

1. Know what your relationship strengths are. List three or four of your relationship strengths:

_____

_____

_____

_____

_____

_____

2. Identify your relationship fears. What keeps you from getting what you want? What prevents you from reaching out to others? Perhaps it is fear of rejection, connection, involvement, or other barriers? Please note some of your relationship fears:

_____

_____

_____

_____

_____

3. Develop your own confidence. Networking involves risk taking as you know. Ask for what you want. Do you remember times when you took a risk, spoke to someone, considered their feelings, and you ended up getting what you wanted? Write down these experiences now so that you begin to acknowledge yourself and your capabilities. What skills did you use?

_____

_____

_____

_____

_____

_____

☑ BOE'S GUIDE #18: Networkers are always able to forgive with love. One of the most difficult processes that people have is the ability to forgive themselves or others who have caused them any emotional, relationship and/or financial pain. To grow and to move on, one has to learn the art of letting go. The networker knows when to walk away with his or her power intact. Remember, you can't give away anything that you don't have so don't lose part of yourself by holding on to old hurts or resentments.

"To be wronged is nothing unless you continue to remember it."
—Confucious

FORGIVENESS PROMOTES A GOOD ATTITUDE

Forgiveness can be an effective and even easy process that will help you communicate with people. The attitudes of resentment or pain or revenge, all lead us to an attitude of dwelling on the past. These historical events are just that—something that does not belong in your future. Invariably, the past prevents us from going forward. To advance toward our goal, we must get rid of the excess baggage—the weight on our shoulders that bogs us down. The key to releasing this negative energy is to forgive. Don't just say the words, but mean it by including the associated feelings, thoughts, and debts. Accept the forgiven person, including yourself, as one who is free and clear of the cause, regardless of whether the person is apologetic or not. The weight is on you because you choose to keep it there. Likewise, it is removed from you only when you choose to let it go. Do not allow the other person to influence the way in which you control your attitudes. Your happiness is a direct result of your choice to be happy.

Forgiveness begins when you are willing to let go of any hurt, guilt, resentment, or attachment to yourself or the person you are forgiving. The next step is to let these negative feelings go because they are not worth holding on to. Some people would rather be right than be happy. They must learn to let hostile feelings go.

The best thing about forgiveness is that it is a way of healing your life. This healing will lead to being able to better communicate with others. This assures your long term success, joy, happiness, and inner peace—the key to all riches.

"Always forgive your enemies—nothing annoys them so much."
—Oscar Wilde

Learn the forgiveness process. If you want great health, wealth, and happiness you must be freely moving forward. Let past hurts and pains go by forgiving yourself and everyone else for whatever has happened or failed to happen. The time to create miracles is now!

AFFIRMATIONS
I am worthy of being forgiven.

I release with love all the past people who may have caused me pain, and for events that were painful.

I release all negative thoughts through forgiving. This will lighten and free my body. I can breath in fresh air and feel alive. There is plenty of room for glorious new experiences.

I live with joy, lightness, and laughter.

SKILL BUILDER

Fill in the blanks:

I forgive myself with love for _____

_____

_____

_____

_____

_____

I forgive (another person) _____

for _____

_____

_____

_____

_____

_____

☑ BOE'S GUIDE #19: Learn to lighten up and laugh at yourself. Networkers know the importance of humor. If you think every communication and relationship is urgent, then you will not enjoy the networking process and you will absolutely stop the growth of your network. The growth and nurturing of your network will determine your business success. List some ways in which you are currently expanding and growing your network through your relationship process:

_____

_____

_____

_____

☑ BOE'S GUIDE #20: Make friends even when you don't need them. Networkers know that the worst time to make a friend is when you need one. I'd hate to be the one to tell you, but when your energy is down, nobody wants to be around you! So you need to build a network of friends beforehand so that when you need a friend, they already exist. Friends are the most precious beings in the whole world. I have more friends now than ever before, and I've never been busier as my networking career continues to expand. Yet I've always taken time to nurture my friend network by saying thank-you, by telling people I appreciate them, and by letting them know how much I care about them.

Bonding power! Nearly all successful people have an extraordinary ability to bond with others by connecting and developing rapport with a variety of backgrounds and beliefs. The great successful families all have the aptitude to form bonds that unite them to millions of others. Deep in the recesses of your heart you need to form lasting, loving bonds with others. Without that, any success, any excellence, is unrewarding and worthless.

SKILL BUILDER

What kind of people do you like to spend time with?

_____

_____

_____

_____

What do such people bring out in you that others do not?

_____

_____

_____

What can people learn about you by looking at your friends?

_____

_____

_____

☑ BOE'S GUIDE #21: Networkers need to give without expectation. It has been said many times that givers receive. Networking begins with an attitude of wanting to share with others. Networkers know that there will be times when they need advice or help, so in turn, they are always willing to give. There are times when giving may not be enough. As an example, a farmer who wants a crop must condition the earth. Next, the farmer must sow or plant the seed or end up with a harvest of only weeds. When you were born, the first thing the doctor did was to hold you upside down by the heels and smack your little bottom. You gave a big wail that started you breathing. Even breathing is an example of giving and receiving. Your life depends on this process. Forgiving with love is your greatest energy renewing force.

The truth is that you must start giving before you can start receiving. This is the kind of universe in which we live. Every time we give we release ever increasing energy that will return to us in a greater magnitude. When you give without expectation, it also serves to fix in your mind the image of the desired return. Expect the unexpected as your gifts may come from many sources.

AFFIRMATIONS

My capacity to receive increases daily. It expands and magnifies.

"Thank you" can make it all work.

I prosper in giving by relaying beneficial, positive, constructive and specific words, and thoughts and emotions. I enjoy giving gifts of services, aid, help, love, praise, encouragement, and even money. I claim my tenfold return on all of these from the infinite as it is both my privilege and my duty.

SKILL BUILDER

Write an incident where you gave and then received much more in return.

_____

_____

_____

_____

_____

Do you feel you have much impact on the lives of people with whom you come in contact?

_____

_____

_____

_____

_____

Can you think of someone who, over a short time, significantly influenced your life?

_____

_____

_____

_____

_____

Networkers always win and always spread joy to other people. Remember, whatever you give out comes back. It may not come back from that person, but it will come back. So remember networkers, be aware and practice these traits. Show examples of how you will incorporate these traits into your life:

Being persistent: _____

_____

_____

_____

Being patient: _____

_____

_____

_____

_____

Learning to ask for what you want with sensitivity and compassion:

_____

_____

_____

_____

_____

Making someone else feel more important: _____

_____

_____

_____

_____

Acknowledging someone else and putting them at ease: _____

_____

_____

_____

_____

Learning to break the ice and do cocktail talk: _____

_____

_____

_____

_____

Enjoying the process: _____

_____

_____

_____

Going through your fear barriers: _____

_____

_____

_____

_____

Networking every day: _____

_____

_____

_____

_____

Saying thank-you for what you have rather than complaining about
what you don't have: _____

_____

_____

_____

Growing and nurturing your network: _____

_____

_____

_____

_____

☑ BOE'S GUIDE #22: Know that one of the greatest human needs
is to be deeply understood and accepted. Networkers always come
from acceptance versus judgment. Make some notes in the following
space to assess yourself concerning your need to be accepted.

What I accept about others is: _____

_____

_____

_____

_____

_____

What I judge and/or reject about others is: _____

_____

_____

_____

_____

Now write your feelings concerning giving understanding and acceptance to others. _____

_____

_____

_____

_____

☑ BOE'S GUIDE #23: Find out what your customers' or clients' needs are and learn to fulfill their needs. Doing business in today's economy means you are able to quickly identify and get into their communication framework rather than your own. Everyone is motivated by their own communication style. Learn to quickly analyze your customer's communication style and then to talk with them on their level.

☑ BOE'S GUIDE #24: Networking is integrative. Make networking part of your lifestyle by working from the inside out. Every day I want you to nurture your network, say thank-you, think about your career and personal goals, and always ask yourself "What's important now?" One of my students in a San Diego class reminded me that the phrase stands for WIN. Networkers most often win in their life because they know how to focus their energy towards what they want, not what they don't want, and it always comes from kindness, as kindness is your greatest reward. Integrating means to merge all aspects of your daily activities into your networking philosophy for the betterment of your lifestyle and the pursuit of your goals.

RESOURCEFULNESS WORKS!

Resourcefulness is more of an attitude than a way of thinking or a way of operating. Looking for opportunities to be resourceful supports the people in your network. Tapping your resources enlivens the spirit, empowering you and your fellow networkers. Take a moment to think of to whom you can give an idea, a referral, or word of support. Take advantage of the skills and expertise around you. Be resourceful and responsive. Look for ways that you can we be supportive. Become a resource to others and allow them to use your expertise. Start living networking—amazing things can happen.

SKILL BUILDER

In the following items, list how you believe resourcefulness can be applied:

Expanding your scope (broadening your network): _____

_____
_____
_____
_____
_____

Enhancing your value to other people: _____

_____
_____
_____
_____
_____

Using the abilities of other networkers: _____

_____
_____
_____
_____
_____

☑ BOE'S GUIDE #25: Networkers know that relationships are your key to business survival and prosperity. Currently in the business world, it is not so much what you know as it is who you know. People like to do business with people they know and like. Always spread your influence and warmth within your business and professional circles so that you are able to find your niche and market yourself. You become your own marketing director as you create your own visibility. List some ways on the lines below in which you create your own visibility and get known by those who count:

_____

_____

_____

_____

_____

☑ BOE'S GUIDE #26: Take time to develop trust with your friends and customers. Trust is the essential ingredient to the networker. You will never have a relationship without trust and rapport. List some ways on the following lines in which you consciously develop trust: _____

_____

_____

_____

☑ BOE'S GUIDE #27: Networkers know how to ask for help. Networkers exhibit strength by asking for what they want. When you assert your desires, you face the fear of rejection and this fear is the main reason that some people do not network. In this economy, to stay ahead in the business game you must throw out that fear. Make your goals stronger than your fears. Replace fear with joy and opportunity. Draw in people, resources, and information that will help you and give you inner strength. You will need confidence to network. The root-word of confidence is "with faith." Do things in your life besides your work that make you feel good about you.

YOUR SAFETY NET

As was stated earlier, your network is your "safety net." It is your emotional support base allowing you to take risks, overcome your fear of rejection and go towards your goals and dreams. That's why we call it a safety net. If you think that everything that happens to you is crucial and you do not have a backup system (your safety net), then you will not take risks. You will stay exactly where you are, you will be ninety years old and you will say, "I wish I would have."

As we begin to develop your emotional safety net, I want to define these areas. Your **inner circle** consists of people whom you may see on a day-to-day basis. They know all about you because they see your habits, hear your opinions, and hear what goes on in your daily life. Your **friend network** consists of people you do not need to see every day and every night, and who don't need to know everything about you, but who will always be available when called upon. Strong bonds between you and your friends are the norm, but it is also possible to have mere acquaintances in your friend network. With your friend net, you have a commitment to make contact. Your **business network** consists of people whom you may work with such as co-workers, customers, chamber of commerce members, convention and visitor bureau members—any professional organization you belong to, any health clubs, churches, and breakfast clubs. It also consists of those acquaintances who are not part of your friend network. The business net is less intimate than the other two networks. Perhaps you may spend less time with these people, however there is still a relationship.

Remember that networking is the ability to structure relationships in your life that are free-flowing, loving, include giving and receiving energy, and allow you to build and go toward your goals. Fill in the following columns with people you feel are, or can be, part of the three types of networks:

YOUR NETWORKING SAFETY NET

INNER CIRCLE	FRIENDS	BUSINESS

After you have completed filling out your three column network that I call your safety net, ask yourself the following questions:

Does my network work for me?   Yes   No

List two strengths of your current network.

_____

_____

List two areas you would like to improve within your network.

_____

_____

Does your network support your current one-year goal that you wrote down and described in Chapter One?   Yes   No
Explain: _____

_____

_____

_____

Does your network include enough people who support you in the way that you emotionally need to be supported?   Yes   No
Comments: _____

_____

_____

_____

The benefits of becoming adept at relating well to others allow you to attract others who appreciate you. Actions have consequences. For example, if you treat people in negative ways, they will act negatively toward you; if you treat people in positive ways, they will act positively toward you. Of course, this sounds simple because it is simple!

When you master human relations, it leads to a win-win situation. Your goodwill will make everyone feel better and eventually will come back to you with interest somewhere down life's road.

To achieve successful human relations, to merely philosophize about them is insufficient; they must be implemented through words and actions. The following are some of the more important traits that must become habits if you are going to master networking skills. The list is not complete but will motivate you to increase your human relations performance.

REMEMBER NAMES. Try to remember names because it makes a person feel good. If you forget a name, you may say, "Forgive me, I'm drawing a blank, I remember your face so well, but for the life of me, I can't remember your name!" Also, state your name to the person with whom you are speaking.

SHOW UP PHYSICALLY AND MENTALLY. Go to as many networking meetings as possible that support your goals. Be present with everyone by taking the energy off you and making someone else the center of your attention.

OPEN UP. You can't just be there, you have to partake. Be yourself, and don't put on a "phony" air. Communicate, show interest, and have fun!

SMILE. It is welcoming and reassuring to others. Smiles are the universal language. A smile is a great opener because the other person doesn't feel rejection.

NOTICE DETAILS. Put your full attention to the person to whom you are conversing. What makes this person interesting and special?

☑ BOE'S GUIDE #28: Networkers help other people win. As you help other people succeed, you not only raise your self-esteem and self-confidence, but you also strengthen relationships. Who doesn't want to be around someone who assists them at the deepest level of satisfying their needs? List on the lines below, some ways that you help your current customers satisfy their needs and assist them in achieving their goals and dreams: _____

_____

_____

_____

_____

_____

☑ BOE'S GUIDE #29: Act like a host or hostess rather than a guest. Networkers know that they have to take the initiative and

often they have to be the risk taker. Think about what a host or
hostess does at a party. The host or hostess will say, "Can I offer
you a drink"; "Can I get you another hors d'oeuvre"; or "Can I
have the pleasure of introducing you to someone." They may not
know you and yet they are taking the risk to break the ice and, of
course, to be the great networker. Act like a host or hostess
wherever you go because this is a fundamental skill of the networker.
Networkers succeed and stay ahead in the business world because
they are pro-active as well as very sensitive.

HOST/HOSTESS BEHAVIOR

Hosts always exhibit gracious manners by meeting people,
making introductions, starting conversations, and making sure that
the needs of others are met. Hosts and hostesses are genuinely
concerned with the comfort of others and actively contribute to that
comfort. You will feel more comfortable by extending yourself to
others and others will be naturally drawn to you.

At this point you should review the reason you are networking
and what benefits of networking you would like to achieve:

I want to be a networker to: _____

_____

_____

_____

I expect to achieve: _____

_____

_____

_____

☑ BOE'S GUIDE #30: Networkers are able to ask interesting
questions. Whenever you break the ice with someone, you should
make them the most important person whether you are with them five
minutes or five years. Networkers succeed in the business world
through their positive attitude and concern for the feelings of others.

Most of the time you can break the ice with small talk. Start
by initially introducing yourself, "Hi, my name is Katy Smith,

with Smith and Jason Law Firm. I handle the transcriptions. I noticed that you are with the Johnson Group. What exactly do you do?" Don't worry if you know nothing about the person or their firm or the goings-on in their environment. Remember, that person is the most important person. Practice the art of being present and the art of showing interest in someone else to quickly develop rapport. Any questions or comments will do. At a networking gathering, your fellow networkers will realize that you are initiating conversation and they will reciprocate. So you could have just as easily said, "I notice you are with the Johnson Group. I've heard that name before, but can't quite place where that was or what it is that your firm does." The natural inclination of your conversant will be to say, "We specialize in corporate tax laws . . ." or some other such response. Your next move is to say, "How interesting! I've always wanted to learn more about . . ." You can see where this leads. Pay attention and listen to what is being said. Often, at a future time, you will need information and recall that this person has the ideal awareness that you seek.

Avoid questions that virtually demand a yes or no answer. If your icebreaker does so, the other person will be helpless to keep it going. So as part of your preparation to network, practice developing open ended questions that pertain to a variety of professions, of hobbies, of politics, and other topics that may be appropriate.

SKILL BUILDER

Think about the last professional networking mixer you attended. Perhaps it was a chamber of commerce function or convention and visitor's bureau mixer. Visualize yourself relating to the people in the room. What question did you use as an icebreaker?

List several questions that require more than a yes or no answer: _____

_____

_____

_____

☑ BOE'S GUIDE #31: Be willing to listen and learn. You can learn through the experiences of others. For example, you can never know too much about your job. You can learn from everybody around you—just keep your eyes and ears open. An example of this is when I observed an associate at a meeting. He was very quiet and not talking at all. He did, however, take in all the information that was being given out. Then, when he finally spoke, he said something very special, intelligent, and meaningful. It was from his heart, using all the information he had gathered. This is a good tip to follow. How you listen and respond is an important skill.

EXERCISE

You probably have been in a situation where you spoke more than you listened. Afterward, you may have felt satisfied that you made your point, but have little recollection of what the thoughts of another were, or what you may have gained if you had listened more. How do you listen and respond?

_____

_____

_____

_____

_____

Would you make any changes in the way you listened and responded to give you more power and clout?

_____

_____

_____

_____

_____

How will you respond when you receive compliments today? The best response is to look someone directly in the eyes and enthusiastically say "Thank you." Next, repeat what you heard so that you can be sure that the compliment sinks into your consciousness. For instance, if an associate says, "That's a great presentation," you can say, "Thank you. I'm glad you liked my presentation because I feel it will be of benefit to everyone in the company." How do you usually respond to a compliment?

_____

_____

_____

_____

Make an effort to say something positive about yourself today to a special friend. If it doesn't seem appropriate to say anything in front of people, stand in front of the mirror and say, "I am a good person" or other confidence building affirmation. What will you say to yourself or a friend?

_____

_____

_____

_____

_____

At the end of the day review your work. Did you do the best you could?

_____

_____

_____

_____

_____

Do you feel comfortable praising yourself?

_____

_____

_____

_____

Do you really believe your thoughts are causing your experiences?

_____

_____

_____

_____

What do you believe about your talents and abilities?

_____

_____

_____

_____

What do you like best about your life?

_____

_____

_____

_____

What do you like least?

_____

_____

_____

_____

AFFIRMATIONS

I create my own positive experiences.

My thoughts are powerful and positive.

I attract wonderful people into my life.

I am a good and loyal friend.

Everyone likes me.

I accept only the best for myself from this moment forward. I accept wealth, excellent health, great relationships, a loving life, and wonderful creative and fun experiences.

As I accept, I can receive. I now accept the best for myself. I open my mind, my heart and eyes to the possibilities of life. This is the first day of the rest of my new life!

I am prosperous; I am successful; I am wealthy.

My additional affirmations:

_____

_____

_____

_____

_____

☑ BOE'S GUIDE #32: Networking is the ability to give as well as receive. When you come from the heart, you always give and you are always nurturing. Networking is a loop. Not only do you give out energy, resources, information, advice, and support; but you also are able to receive exactly what you need. You earn the right to have a friend and you earn the right to do business with someone. Do not rush relationships. We are finally a networking community and I'm proud to say that I am at the right place at the right time with my keynote, motivational speaking business! Never give up—success is right around the corner!

☑ BOE'S GUIDE #33: Communication is a tool to be used effectively. Use clear and appropriate requests, organize your thoughts, and develop a speaking style that is easy to listen to and easy to understand. We can learn to match the style and tempo of those with whom we are conversing. We must also practice communication skills. Much more than speaking or words, these skills also include: tone, content, body and facial expressions, and perhaps most importantly, the ability to listen. Hear what is being said, not just the sound of the words. Strive to listen seventy-five (75%) to eighty percent (80%) of your time, reducing downward toward fifty percent (50%) only when so invited by your conversant. Another skill to listening is to give reinforcement to what was said. Show body language to what the other person said to show your genuine interest. For example, a nod of the head or the raising of an eyebrow can communicate effectively without stealing the show.

Be mindful of your voice qualities. It is difficult to talk to someone who has a squeaky voice, high-pitched voice, or who comes across with a nasal tone. Also, it is undesirable to keep a conversation going with someone who is a "know it all," or who is a whiner or complainer. Who wants to hear it! So from your perspective, become a pleasant person with whom to chat.

EXERCISE

Write down a small, typical conversation, with both parties parts. Then, using a small tape recorder, "read" the parts, just as if you are an actor in a play with a cocktail party scene. Finally, listen to how you sound. Many people are astonished at hearing their recorded voice, usually making a comment like, "I had no idea that this is how I sound!"

Evaluate your voice tones objectively, and strive to "repair" those deficiencies that you feel you have. This simple exercise will allow you to improve your conversation skills, feel better about yourself, and greatly improve your self-confidence that, in turn, will enable you to become a much better conversant. Is your pitch too high? If so, practice speaking from lower within the diaphragm. Is your pace too fast, appearing almost "hyperactive?" Then slow your pace to a more deliberate, thought provoking style. Do you feel the pace to be too slow, bordering on being boring? Then practice increasing your rate or shortening your sentences. Are you too terse or brief? Then work on expanding your sentences by adding opinions, observations, or other facts to make you appear to be more well versed. If your voice comes across in a harsh tone, soften it. You get the idea—now take action.

Write down observations about your current voice qualities:

_____

_____

_____

_____

_____

Now itemize improvements that you may feel are necessary:

_____

_____

_____

_____

☑ BOE'S GUIDE #34: Clean up your communications quickly. Any withholding of energy creates a barrier between you and your customers. Approximately fifty-five percent (55%) of all your communications are non-verbal. When you stand in front of someone, they get a positive feeling about you as you do with them. It is very important that you totally show up! Write down on the lines below, anything that may be keeping you from being one hundred percent (100%) persent with your customers:

_____

_____

_____

Anytime that somebody is inappropriate to you in a communication sense, do not belabor the conversation. Be polite and recognize that further discussion is wasting your time and your partner's. There are other encounters waiting for each of you. Use their name and say, "Thank you for sharing that with me" and get out of their energy.

BREVITY

Experience has taught me that when you're dealing with successful networkers, you are always aware that their time is a valuable asset. You will gain respect when you can quickly organize and communicate your thoughts. Therefore, when you have something to say, be succinct and keep it simple by saying exactly what you mean.

Positive information is much better received if presented in a brief manner. Even negative information will be less painful if it isn't dragged out. When you are trying to communicate with someone, organize the following issues that need to be addressed:

Why am I communicating this information?

What will the receiver do with the information? If we accomplish everything we hope to, specifically how can we create a win-win situation?

☑ BOE'S GUIDE #35: Networkers know never to break the knots in their net. There will be times that you are dealing or conversing with a person, and you know that the direction is not right. Perhaps the other person is filled with negative energy at that time. Anytime that somebody is inappropriate to you at a particular time in a communication sense, conclude the communication but not the relationship. Tactfully say, "Thank you for sharing that with me. Now I must be getting on to other business." Do not be negative or terse, but continue to get out of their energy! You'll find that these people may come back to you in the future as your career grows and strengthens, so why break a trust. Do not give them a reason to avoid future relationships. List below a time when you stepped out of the way of a less than positive situation and later had the person come back into your network. _____

_____

_____

_____

RELATIONSHIPS GROW

Relationships grow and sometimes they become stronger, and sometimes the links become weaker but you always want to keep the knots together. You will want to take a look at your network and see if there are any holes, any needs of repair, and any people you need to nurture. Remember, networking always begins with an attitude and always begins with you valuing yourself enough that you can value someone else. It is absolutely impossible to have a relationship if you do not think you are worthy. You will actually push people away. This will be done subconsciously and the only way you may discover this is if your net is not working. Always ask yourself: is your net working personally and professionally? By staying connected to your inner self and your inner voice, which some call intuition, you will always stay on the right track of your networking. From your intuition, know your own truths. You want to assess if your relationships are supporting your personal or career goal or goals.

☑ BOE'S GUIDE #36: Always say, "Thank-you." Networking is the ability to acknowledge other people for the smallest of kindnesses. Always remember that kindness is its greatest reward. Now list some ways in which you are able to be kind and to thank other people in your network: _____

_____

_____

_____

_____

_____

ACKNOWLEDGING WHAT IS

Speak what you see and what you feel. Acknowledge strengths wherever they exist. Acknowledge your successes no matter how small. Make it part of your day, as this simple and powerful tool provides a very valuable reinforcement system and keeps your energy level high. Notice what others are doing. It is natural to be wise and give positive strokes. Take advantage of your many opportunities. Be sincere, spontaneous, and generous. Acknowledge to yourself and to others, in writing and verbally. Look to each person to see what is appropriate and most effective for that person. Develop a system or structure, thank-you cards, simple note reminders and acknowledgments, and send it along the way. Take time at the end of work as the work is completed. Telephone calls are even more effective at times than a thank-you note because the listener can hear the sincerity in your voice. Look forward to the opportunity to acknowledge your gains. Don't take relationships for granted and show an attitude of gratitude. Keep relationships alive and well. Don't look for credit for yourself it will come when you least expect it. Give others credit whenever possible, and be happy to give support. Be sure to say, "Thanks for the phone call, the lead, and for thinking of me."

SKILL BUILDER

If you were to have a gratitude party, how many people would you invite? Complete the following invitation for eight of your friends:

(name) _____,

You are invited to a gratitude party! You are an honorable and special guest. I am especially appreciative of _____

_____

_____

_____

_____

_____

(name) _____,
You are invited to a gratitude party! You are an honorable and special guest. I am especially appreciative of _____

_____

_____

_____

_____

_____

(name) _____,
You are invited to a gratitude party! You are an honorable and special guest. I am especially appreciative of _____

_____

_____

_____

_____

_____

(name) _____,
You are invited to a gratitude party! You are an honorable and special guest. I am especially appreciative of _____

_____

_____

_____

_____

_____

(name) _____,
You are invited to a gratitude party! You are an honorable and special guest. I am especially appreciative of _____

_____

_____

_____

_____

_____

(name) _____,
You are invited to a gratitude party! You are an honorable and
special guest. I am especially appreciative of _____

_____

_____

_____

_____

_____

(name) _____,
You are invited to a gratitude party! You are an honorable and
special guest. I am especially appreciative of _____

_____

_____

_____

_____

_____

(name) _____,
You are invited to a gratitude party! You are an honorable and
special guest. I am especially appreciative of _____

_____

_____

_____

_____

_____

Networkers know that everything in life is a relationship and
networking is a learned skill. Not everyone is a natural at relating
to other people. Be natural at having an attitude of gratitude. Wake
up every day and say "Thank-you" for what you have.

Think about the following and answer how you relate to each:

I have a positive attitude.

I am calm and courteous.

I am enthusiastic.

I get respect.

I listen well.

I take criticism as being constructive.

I am cheerful.

I keep an open mind.

I am cooperative.

I improve my performance on a regular basis.

I like others.

I keep personal problems at home.

I have good concentration.

I have integrity.

I quickly develop rapport.

I build trust easily.

I create loyal relationships.

I add value to others.

I acknowledge others' strengths.

I look for good in others.

I find life rewarding, fun, and joyful!

SHOW UP . . . TODAY!

Woody Allen says, "Eighty percent of success in life is showing up." Networkers, you have to show up physically as well as mentally. Remember a time when you were talking to a customer and you wanted to say to him or her, "looks like your lights are on, but nobody's home!" You wanted to knock them on the forehead and see if there was any life left within that person. Of course, you didn't do that because networkers are sensitive. Yet you felt that desire. You wanted to say, "Wake up and live now! This is not a dress rehearsal. Life begins now. I will never have a second chance on today." The only moment that matters is what's going on between you and me right now. Not what happened yesterday, and not what's going to happen tomorrow, but right now. Out of kindness and compassion, of course, we don't do that.

Networkers never miss a moment. Every person you meet is important to you—it's not about what you can get, it's about what you can give. Think of yourself as a lifelong traveler and wherever you go, you are making friends by being open, saying "Thank-you," and following up. Networkers know the advantage of always nurturing their network and having an attitude of gratitude. There is so much to be thankful for. Start the day feeling wonderful by waking up and saying, "Thank-you for what I have!" Never consider wasting energy on what you don't have.

4
NETWORKING CHANGES YOUR FUTURE!

*"Through your preparation and intent
you can get whatever you want."*

Out of work? Want a new job? Want to start your own business?
Can you imagine Dorothy, from the Wizard of Oz, losing her job?
You've heard her say, "Lions and tigers and bears, oh my!" Now
it would be, "Résumés and interviews and phone calls, oh my!"
Losing a job can be seen as a turbulent time in one's life. Perhaps
you have a good job, but you feel that you're stagnating. It may be
time to move on or move up. You feel as though you are helplessly
swept up in the whirlwind of a tornado, desperately hoping to safely
land somewhere in your customary comfort zone. While the out-
come may not be according to the Land of Oz, you may feel "blown
away" by these changes. It is reassuring to know that in times like
this you have choices and can regain control of your life. Networking can be the safety net to effectively cushion your landing.

CHANGES AND CHANGES, OH MY!

The changes in many people's lives occur with the increase of
layoffs due to economic slowdowns, mergers and acquisitions, and

business reductions. It is mandatory to have networks in place. You may find yourself unemployed, or seeking an advancement, or even doing something entirely different. John A. Artise, in *The Networker's Guide, National Business Employment Weekly*, states that networking is still the way to get a better job: "out placement counselors estimate more than seventy percent (70%) of job seekers, particularly on the executive level, connect new positions through the subtle art of networking." Now more than ever we need to start using the networking process of developing skills and making contacts and developing long, fun, win-win relationships.

NETWORKING AND CRITICAL JOB HUNTING SKILLS

The way you treat networking contacts may determine not only their immediate impact on your career, but also how much they will be available to help you in the future. Most people in this situation would start looking through the want ads in newspapers, trade publications, or may contact an employment agency. There is a possibility that you can land a position through these means, but I strongly feel that you can enhance your chances enormously, and connect with a much more desirable situation, if you use your network connections. You will find that your fellow networkers will have access to leads, or will have heard from other networkers of a need that you can pursue. They can become the key that unlocks the door to your future. When you go through the want ads you compete with many "off the street" candidates who will work for less, and you are no better off than the next person. Furthermore, you may get the response, "Fill out the application and we'll get back to you." You know that the likely next contact is, "Sorry, but we'll keep your résumé on file if our needs change." Who needs that? You can have an "in" with recommendations, referrals, and direct connections to the correct people through your network. Nurture your network, keep it current, and then use it well.

WHY NETWORKING POSITIVELY INCREASES YOUR CHANCES!

Who you know and what you know can have great importance whether you are self-employed or working for a company. Sure, changes involve taking risks and making choices. Reaching your goals will make it all worthwhile. Let's look at your chances for making a career change. Surveys reveal that if you are seeking employment, nearly eighty percent (80%) of all jobs filled in the United States are not known to the general public. This leaves twenty percent (20%) of the jobs that will be divided among the want ads, the employment agencies, executive job search firms, or people finding jobs through just plain luck. As you can see, if you restrict yourself to conventional public sources or luck, you severely reduce your chances of getting the job you want or making those important business contacts that will lead to your success. When you start increasing your base of contacts, coupled with a sense of personal integrity and credibility, networking becomes the most effective process. Here are some reasons:

• Numbers can be in your favor. To increase your odds of making important contacts, meet as many people as you can. You may develop a personal introduction.

• The second underlying theory of why a networking referral works is that people want to assist a dedicated, well-thought-of individual. To do otherwise could be seen as a personal or professional affront to the person who has made the referral. This creates an opening for you that may never have been realized through cold calling.

• Referral networking also builds rapport because someone has endorsed you and believes in you. It takes the guess work out of initial meetings. You become a "known" person to someone and he or she becomes open to listening to you.

EXERCISE

Are you happy with your work or non-work situation?

_____

_____

_____

_____

_____

How do you perceive your ideal work environment?

_____

_____

_____

_____

What short-term work environment changes can you make?

_____

_____

_____

_____

How will you make these changes?

_____

_____

_____

_____

When will you make these changes?

_____

_____

_____

_____

How do you visualize your career or work environment in one year? _____

_____

_____

_____

_____

Two years?

_____

_____

_____

_____

Five years?

_____

_____

_____

_____

Have you considered the pros and cons of owning your own business? List the pros and cons.

Pros: _____

_____

_____

_____

_____

Cons: _____

_____

_____

_____

_____

With over fifty percent (50%) of our economy consisting of small businesses, more and more people are choosing self-employment. In spite of a bleak economic outlook, business opportunities do exist. This is particularly true for creative services, and for those who are willing to go it alone, work in small groups, or in intentional communities. Those who are thinking of being part of a small community might want to consider setting up a cottage industry as a way of funding the community. For example, counseling, writing, teaching, handcrafted items, art, software, accounting, consulting, baking, herbs, and similar functions—these involve personal energy, a commodity that is yours alone. The important thing is to keep your energy in proper perspective and have it match your lifestyle and values. Be gentle to yourself and your business. Business will function best if operated on an intuitive level, with the use of networking and with a good dose of common sense.

IDENTIFY YOUR HIDDEN DREAMS—LIFE WILL BECOME A MORE EXCITING JOURNEY

If your current position is the right one for the moment, that's great. If it doesn't, then start looking for a change—otherwise, you may find yourself in the same rut forever. The definition of a rut is simply a grave open at either end. It's time to identify your hidden dreams so that life can become a more exciting journey.

First we need to analyze your current job or occupation. Answer the following questions:

Does my current job or occupation offer me room for growth?

_____

_____

_____

What kind of advancement might I expect—a better title, a raise, or more responsibilities?

_____

_____

_____

Is this a job that makes me happy?

_____

_____

_____

Will I still be happy five or ten years from now?

_____

_____

_____

Is there some other kind of work I would rather do? If so, explain: _____

_____

_____

_____

Is there another company or occupation that would be more beneficial to my future?

_____

_____

_____

_____

Do I take the extra time to do a good job?

_____

_____

_____

_____

Would I be happier if I had my own business? If so, what kind?

_____

_____

_____

_____

WHAT TYPE OF WORK MAKES YOU HAPPIEST?

Here is an exercise that has been quite successful. Before you start, ask yourself this question: Did you end up in your current profession because someone else suggested that you do so? Did you take the position because of the pay or because of the pleasure? Do you feel that there is a certain amount of danger in changing directions? If so, do you feel that you may end up regretting the change?

Before you decide to take on a career change, or to stay put in your current situation, realize that an ideal situation is one that you enjoy. Every day you should be able to look forward to getting your workday started. If you can't be enthusiastic about starting the day, then surely you should consider a change. If you love your work but feel less than fulfilled financially, then you may want to consider an upgrade within your environment, or a change of employer (perhaps to your own business) within the same industry. The best solution for most people is to do things you like, be good at them, and be sufficiently recognized for your efforts. Here are some samples of things you may like to do: read, take walks, make money, take vacations, talk on the phone. Some samples of things you may be good at include: working with art, dealing with people, organizing, working on the computer, or writing. Fill in the following chart by listing whatever comes to mind on either side of the page:

Things I Like to Do: Things I'm Good At:

Now take a look at what you have written and see if you can connect a line between one or more items on the left with one or more items on the right. If you can, you may find two thirds of the formula come into view—doing something you like and doing it well. What's left of the formula is finding a way to get recognition for your efforts. That's where networking can assist you. Your fellow networkers can enable you to connect with an environment where those skills will be rewarded. Bring as much of yourself as possible into your work!

A BEGINNING—KNOW YOURSELF . . .

Know yourself—know what you want. Know what effort it will take so that you don't get discouraged prematurely, if ever. You will need to do certain things to accomplish your career change. By acknowledging these individual steps, each one will appear small, whereas if you don't envision each small step, the challenge will appear virtually insurmountable. You should know exactly why you are making the change, and where you intend to go. The destination and each of the small steps along the way are goals. You must define these goals before you start your journey, or you could be traveling in the wrong direction. You must decide to pursue these goals. The clearer the goal is, the more likely it will come about. If you are an aerospace engineer and want to find a similar position in a similar company, your activities will be quite different than they would be if you are a financial planner looking for a marketing job. Whatever your situation, you should clearly define both long-term and short-term goals, and do it in writing. This may be much more difficult than you would think, but it's well worth the trouble.

GOALS

Setting goals and defining the plan to accomplish them is a very simple procedure. Granted, you may not have felt that way until now. Our past impressions of goal-setting probably included some lengthy procedure that was complicated and intricate, and resulted in a high probability that the goal was more a dream than something achievable. Do you remember your parents saying, "Don't you want to be the president someday?" That goal, for all but a few, was always felt to be unattainable. So goals, to many of us, were equated to something unattainable. So it is important to define goals that are, with the proper preparation and work, very much achievable. By saying, "Don't you want to be the president of your own company?" you can envision doing so quite easily, providing that your company size and complexity are within your ability to oversee and control. You could direct multiple departments, each with their own manager who reports to you. You could manage your own coffee cart—not much different from the lemonade stand you ran as a child, though on a higher scale and with much more volume. So you see, you can do it if you set your mind to it.

Goals are long-term (e.g., your five year expectations) and short-term (what you plan to accomplish this month or this week). Intermediate goals also exist, but these are more like stepping-stones to the long-term goals.

LONG-TERM GOALS

It is best to define the long-term goal first—this is usually a duration of five years or longer, and can even be retirement oriented. If you've clearly articulated your long-term goal, the intermediate and short-term goals are easy since they are the things necessary to get to your long-term goal. On the other hand, if your long range plans are less clear to you now, then concentrate on specific things you want to get accomplished early on; for example, lose ten pounds by the end of the month. By putting together several short-term goals, you often position yourself to go after something in the future that you may not have thought of previously because you thought it was unattainable or you thought you weren't able to achieve it.

There are no limitations in the long-term goal category. Don't worry about what others may say concerning your goals. You and your subconscious mind determine these and they are not to be shared with others unless you so choose. Many times, by telling another person, you put yourself in a better position to ensure that the goal is met—you have to save face and reputation now that someone else is aware. If a goal is not expressed to another, or in writing, it has an easy chance of being forgotten. Don't be concerned with HOW you will accomplish these big dreams. If you really want them, just write them down. Your mind and my suggestions will show you how later. I am telling you that you can have everything you want out of life if you believe in yourself.

Here are some examples of long-term goals:
- *Have income in excess of $200,000 per year.*
- *Have a career that includes frequent travel.*
- *Finish a graduate program by my 26th birthday.*
- *Fall in love with the person of my dreams.*

Again, don't worry about the number of items you list today. More ideas will come to you later. Doesn't it feel good to be dreaming? Eventually you will have to give up these dreams because they will become realities. In defining your long-term goals, there are important questions that need to be carefully considered and answered:

Am I doing what I really want to be doing?

_____

_____

_____

_____

What would I rather be doing?

_____

_____

_____

_____

How would you describe an ideal working day that would make you happy? _____

_____
_____
_____
_____
_____
_____

What do you envision to be an ideal type of position?

_____
_____
_____
_____
_____
_____
_____

Write a job description.

_____
_____
_____
_____
_____
_____
_____

Where do I see a person like me fitting in this (field, company, industry)? _____

_____
_____
_____
_____
_____

Do I have the necessary skills for this job? If not, what do I need?

_____

_____

_____

_____

_____

Do my qualifications contain any gaps or areas where I could better my skills? _____

_____

_____

_____

_____

What kind of compensation could I expect in the first year?

_____

_____

_____

_____

Is there easy access to promotions and salary increases?

_____

_____

_____

_____

Is my network in place?

_____

_____

_____

_____

SHORT-TERM GOALS

Setting short-term goals is somewhat easier, in that they are simple tasks that can be quantified. These are goals you would like to achieve in the very near future, for example, the next thirty days. Some of these could be personal goals and aren't difficult. A sample of short-term goals may include:

- *Lose five pounds this month.*
- *Finish an important project by the end of the week.*
- *Volunteer three hours at a favorite charity each week.*
- *Make two network contact calls each day.*

NOTE: Be conservative with some of your short-term goals. It is very important for the subconscious to experience immediate success. This will establish in your mind an attitude that success is possible and that you can achieve your goals. Now it's your turn. Please write down a few short-term goals that you desire.

_____

_____

_____

_____

_____

_____

_____

_____

_____

_____

INTERMEDIATE GOALS

These goals cover a period beyond thirty days but no more than one year. As an example:

- *Find a new job within sixty days.*
- *Purchase a new car within two months.*
- *Move to a new home within one year.*
- *Pay off a loan within six months.*

See what I mean? Notice how a time limit is attached to intermediate goals? This is because these goals are not immediate enough to be accomplished today, and without specifying a time limit, you may have a tendency to keep them off in the distance indefinitely. Go ahead and write down the goals you would like to accomplish during the next year.

SETTING YOUR NETWORKING GOALS

There is no doubt that networking for a job is a "numbers game," and that the more contacts you make, the sooner you'll succeed. Reports from the top out placement firms indicated that among people who are unemployed, the ones who succeed in finding a new job complete five network telephone calls per day and two network interviews. Obviously, if you're currently employed and looking for a job on the side, you won't be able to make as many contacts. Still, you should set yourself specific short-term goals to make some phone calls and inquiries, and strive for some face-to-face contacts after work.

CHECK YOUR GOALS

At this point it's important that you stop for a moment and check the generalities you have written. To be achievable, and thus productive for your future, a goal must meet certain criteria. Look at each single generality you have written and check it against the questions on the next page:

• Is it my goal? It cannot be something that someone else wants for you. Your goals must come from your heart and you must have the belief that these goals may have started out as dreams but will become realistic, achievable goals. Furthermore, when you achieve your goal, you must be glad you did so.

• Will the goal conflict with my family or close friends? It would be difficult to accomplish a goal that would cause a drastic conflict with people who are close to you. If there is a conflict, have a discussion and try to resolve the matter.

• Is it a positive goal? Let's stay away from any negative.

• Am I excited about achieving this goal? Be reasonable when establishing your goals, and make them truly desirable.

• Is the goal big enough? Make sure your goal will be enough of a challenge to interest you.

• Is it financially in line with my other goals? If you desire a Porsche, your goals to cause it to materialize should show a sufficient income to allow money for the purchase.

Review your goals to make sure that they are stated in specific detail and make sure that each goal is written as if it were already accomplished. Don't say, "I hope I have a new car next spring." It won't happen because you have already started the creative force toward the uncertainty. Rather, say, "I will have my new red Corvette convertible by my next birthday, June 3, 1994." Then, go make it happen.

WORKING AFFIRMATIONS ARE POWERFUL

Go through your short-term goals and determine your top choice. Now transform generalities into working affirmations. For instance the goal of making a career change should be stated in a positive affirmation as if it has already been accomplished and in specific details with a date. Acknowledge the power of your affirmation by recording the accomplishment. A sample affirmation may look like this: It's July 30, 1994. I have changed my career and now have more time to enjoy life and make more money. I feel fantastic!

By stating your affirmation with specifics, such as the completion date, and your emotions (the way you feel), your subconscious mind will perceive that the affirmation has already happened. Go back and make affirmations for each of your goals. Don't forget to give specific details about each goal and to state the target date and emotion felt. Please do not make your affirmations long—be precise and concise.

To get somewhere in life, you must have feelings about where you want to go and how you want to be. That is precisely what you are doing here. What makes networking so exciting and rewarding is that you are writing down what you want out of life. Congratulations on finding your truth and on getting focused. You are a winner!

TOP DOWN OR BOTTOM UP?

Do you know how to get your goals accomplished? You do so through planning and action. You know how to take action, but do you know how to plan? You can't just say, "I plan to make a fortune." You may have a goal to make a fortune, but the plan must contain specific actions that have to be accomplished along a timeline. The intermediate steps along the timeline are called milestones, and you should strive to closely monitor your milestones to ensure that you are progressing on schedule, according to your plan. Thus, you can make adjustments promptly so that your overall goal continues to be attainable.

Where do you start? What do you put on your plan first? What sequence must your actions be in? These are all questions that can cause an average person to procrastinate or give up entirely. This symptom can be avoided through an approach that clearly defines the individual steps. Two such approaches exist: a top down approach or a bottom up approach.

TOP DOWN IS VISIONARY

Visualize a pyramid. At the top is your long-term goal. The stones at the bottom are your short-term goals. As you climb the pyramid toward the top, you are advancing toward the long-term destination. Since you know where it is that you are heading, you can see that each of the stones along the way is in direct support of the stone at the top. As you achieve each of the intermediate goals, you are solidifying your foundation for the achievement of your goal.

The **top down approach** is the approach you should strive for, since it is the more likely to result in success. In this approach, you first define your long-term goal. Accurately define the appropriate components necessary to have that goal. Then, treating each of those components as separate entities, define the sub-components necessary for each. As you can envision with the pyramid, you are starting at the top and determining what supporting element is necessary at each successive level below. As an example, presume that your long-term goal is to be the president of your own craft store. This is the top of the pyramid. Envision what components are necessary—an appropriate location, adequate materials, a well-trained staff, and a sound business operation. Now take each of those items as a goal in itself and define the pieces for each. For example, for the business operation you will need an attractive business name, an accounting system, bank accounts, business license, marketing materials, sound financing, and other items of this nature. The same applies to location, materials, and staff. Then parse further until you have many small steps, such as "open a bank account." Obviously, each of the small steps can be accomplished easily, and all that is necessary is to define when (your timeline of milestones). Then start the process into motion.

BOTTOM UP CAN BE FASCINATING

With a **bottom up approach**, a person is not always sure exactly where it is that they want to end up eventually. For example, ask most high school students what they want to be when they "grow-up" and you'll find that very few know the exact answer. Many will have a general idea, such as "something in the medical field." With the bottom up approach, you take those things you do well and use them. You take the short-term goals and as they are accomplished, build upon them. In a sense, you are laying out the stones of the foundation, the lowest level of the pyramid, and then finding the stones to put upon them. The problem with this approach, which is why I encourage the top down if at all possible, is that you don't always know what you will end up with, and you may find yourself having to start all over! Your vision is obviously cloudy if you choose this approach, but it can lead you into new and fascinating directions that you may not have come across if you had focused on a single, nebulous long-term goal.

As an example of the bottom up approach, consider that you are good at crafts, but hadn't considered it more than just a hobby. Your short-term goals may have included changing your appearance, becoming more active in your network, and expressing a desire to break loose from your nine-to-five secretarial job. So you tackle the short-term goals by voicing your interests to your fellow networkers. Among the conversations, a networker asks if your crafts include sewing, as that person has heard of a related opening dealing with overseeing hand-made dresses. Taking this position, you acquire skills that are unique to the industry, and when coupled with your change in appearance, you find that you are asked to represent your company at the dress trade shows. Then through new network relationships associated with the shows, you connect with a dress designer firm who entices you to use your creative skills and knowledge of dress-making at their firm in Los Angeles. As you can see, the bottom up approach led to a career as a dress designer, something you may never have envisioned when you sat at your secretarial desk.

POWER PLANNING

It is obvious that for networking to work for your career, your efforts must not be haphazard. They must be planned to achieve the desired results. Job hunters and career advancers need to take the initiative to actively seek out opportunities and convert obstacles into challenges and opportunities. By having identified a sound plan and by taking action, job seekers can make new contacts, uncover job leads, and persuade employers to hire them. Through persistence and determination, they can overcome hiring obstacles. Power planning is the ability to find and weigh facts, to be objective, and to exercise sound judgment. Your individual plan will consist of steps specific to your goals, both short-term and long-term. As a part of any plan you must prioritize your contacts, do your networking letters and calls, update your résumé, be prepared mentally for interviews, and have a conviction about what you want to achieve. The following formula can end with outstanding results:

- **Understand the challenge;** the need to find a new job. Study and be aware of all the facts.
- **State the challenge in question form.** Be concise and clear. How am I going to do all this?
- **Define the issues.** Weigh the advantages, disadvantages, and all the alternatives. I can create a professional image if I do this correctly.
- **State your conclusions.** Be definite. I will follow ideas about these issues and solicit suggestions from fellow networkers to help round out my conclusions.
- **Give reasons for your conclusions.** I want a career change that will make everyone happy and prosperous—a win-win situation.
- **Take action.** I will start today at step one and have my résumé, network letter, organization skills and follow-up ready within six days.

Just as you should "Think before speaking,"
you should "Plan before acting."

SO, HOW DO I MARKET MYSELF?

You may have decided to alter your career objectives, and need to know the best way to approach marketing yourself. By far, the single biggest factor that can slow down a job search is wasting time with job sources that are known to produce little result. Thus, job searchers may waste as much as 80% to 90% of their time focusing on sources and techniques such as want ads, placement offices, computer résumé matching services, and so on, that statistically account for less than 5% of the jobs that are found. For most people in this situation, this is the normal starting point. My advice to you is to use these vehicles only after you have used your network. Chances are likely that you will never have to investigate a newspaper ad!

You are your number one special person. Be proud of yourself, and let your fellow networkers realize that you are special. Devise a "weekly planner" of your near-term contacts, prioritizing according to your goals, defining frequency of contacts, and follow-up schedule. The networking contacts can be in person or by phone, and are not limited to the following categories. Can you list some names in each category?

Family Members

_____   _____
_____   _____
_____   _____
_____   _____

Friends

_____   _____
_____   _____
_____   _____
_____   _____

Neighbors

_____   _____
_____   _____
_____   _____
_____   _____

Acquaintances

_____   _____
_____   _____
_____   _____

Employers

_____   _____
_____   _____
_____   _____
_____   _____
_____   _____

Co-workers

_____   _____
_____   _____
_____   _____
_____   _____
_____   _____

Insurance Brokers

_____   _____
_____   _____
_____   _____
_____   _____
_____   _____

Doctors

_____   _____
_____   _____
_____   _____
_____   _____
_____   _____

Lawyers

_____   _____
_____   _____
_____   _____
_____   _____
_____   _____

Alumni

_____   _____
_____   _____
_____   _____
_____   _____
_____   _____

Clergy

_____   _____
_____   _____
_____   _____
_____   _____
_____   _____

Accountants

_____   _____
_____   _____
_____   _____
_____   _____
_____   _____

Club Members

_____   _____
_____   _____
_____   _____
_____   _____
_____   _____

Charities

_____   _____
_____   _____
_____   _____
_____   _____
_____   _____

Others

_____   _____
_____   _____
_____   _____
_____   _____
_____   _____

By starting with personal contacts, you will feel the most comfortable and be able to get needed networking experience. The next step will be to let these people know your intentions. There's a paradox in networking for a job: You can't overtly state your objective to the people you contact. This is because no one likes to be put on the spot by being asked for a job. You should be tuned-in to the right time and method of calling upon your contacts. If your relations are based on trust, compassion and understanding, your contacts will be willing to help you. Remember, it's easy for a contact to misunderstand the networker's intention. Many people assume that a person planning a job change is asking for a job. You must let each contact know that you are not putting them on the spot, or asking them to be your personal headhunter but would appreciate them keeping you in mind if they come across any openings that may interest you.

IDENTIFYING TARGET COMPANIES

With your goal in mind, your résumé prepared, and a start on making known contacts, the next step is to identify those companies where you would like to work, and where your skills and experience would most likely be in demand. Your local library contains a wealth of information for you to target companies and identify the specific people within those corporations you want to meet. You should target at a level high enough to hire you, but don't neglect peers for higher-ups. Once you have identified your targets, ask everyone you contact, "Do you know anyone at XYZ company who might know her?" or, "Do you have any contacts at the ABC company?" Note that it's important to give people a chance to think. Whenever you ask about further contacts, don't speak until the other person has responded.

Targeting is a good technique because it's efficient and keeps you pointed toward your goal. However, it does have its drawbacks. Typically, you'll end up targeting the larger, better known companies, where competition for jobs is stiffer. Your time is limited, so focusing on large, well-known companies will detract from your efforts with smaller companies, as well as companies you simply didn't consider. For this reason, I recommend that you consider spending a certain amount of time "shot-gunning." Pursuing companies or people that aren't central to your strategy can sometimes bring unexpected positive results. This type of networking can also be of great value even after you've found a job.

RÉSUMÉ COVER: THE INITIAL CONTACT

The first thing that a person sees when you submit your résumé is the cover letter. It should be written to capture their attention. Do not just introduce it with standard words that invite "here it is, file it in your six month file." As a minimum you must state your intentions, such that you are submitting your résumé for consideration, you believe your experience and qualifications would enable you to contribute to the growth and prosperity of their company, and that you would appreciate the opportunity to discuss your capabilities in person. Also add some teasers why you are someone that should be moved to the top of their list of candidates. These can be derived by tailoring your cover letter to each recipient.

If you use a "plain vanilla, generic" cover letter, you will be viewed in the same light. If, on the other hand, you use your networking connections to learn specifics about the recipient, you can add uniqueness to your cover letter. For example, use an individual's name or specific projects or specific duties. This will allow your résumé to get to the correct person and increase the likelihood that the person will want to meet with you. "I have been told that Mr. Johnson is seeking help in the research department. I have recently finished a similar task that would be very useful on the XYZ project . . ." As you can see, you have a much better chance than if you said "if you have anything that might fit what I do." Make your image fit their need, not vice versa. Finally, make sure they know that you are going to follow-up by stating that you will be contacting them soon to see when (not if) they would like to schedule an interview.

The important thing is to be understood. Find out as much about the position as possible, and know to whom you are writing. Place yourself in the reader's position. Remember, there is something very final about a letter, therefore use the following rules:

• **Be friendly**. Your letters should be cordial without being too familiar. Keep in good taste.

• **Be brief**. Get to the heart of the matter quickly. Avoid fancy and unnecessary words.

• **Be thorough**. Anticipate and answer potential questions now to avoid follow-up correspondence.

• **Be sincere**. Stay away from clichés.

• **Review and re-write**. Even professional writers don't get it correct the first time.

WORD POWER IN BUSINESS WRITING CHECKLIST

Ask yourself the following questions:

• Does the opening sentence get to the heart of the matter quickly?

• Are thoughts arranged in logical order?

• Is it clear what you expect of the reader?

• Does the correspondence have a "YOU" attitude?

• Have you used active words instead of passive words?

• Is the grammar and punctuation correct?

• Does the letter read smoothly and have a good appearance?

RÉSUMÉS THAT GETS RESULTS

Update your résumé! You should always have your résumé ready before you start to network. Your contacts will often ask to see it, either to review it if there is a current opening, or to send it to an associate in another department or company. Make sure your résumé is ready ahead of time, well organized, and oriented toward your accomplishments. Don't just appear to be a worker—make yourself look like an achiever.

WHAT NOT TO DO IN THE NAME OF NETWORKING

Consider the following network introduction. "Good morning, Mr. Smith. John Foley gave me your name. I'm looking for a position as a financial consultant and was wondering if you have an opening." This approach forces Mr. Smith to immediately say no. This ends any opportunity you would have had to spend time with him, get valuable information, and perhaps even impress him to the point where he would want to hire you. Even if he happens to be looking for an engineer on the day you call, he's likely to ask you to send a résumé and will put your name in the same pile with dozens of other job seekers.

Now consider this introduction. "Good morning, Mr. Smith. A mutual friend of ours, John Foley, asked me to give you a call. He said that you need some help in your financial department and thought of me since I have financial consulting experience. If you need some help, I would be happy to see if I can assist as a favor to you and John." Most likely, Mr. Smith will counter with something like, "Well, thanks for the offer, but we really need someone who is willing to work for us full-time." Then, you can open the door by saying, "I see. Well, in that case I can come in and discuss your needs with you, and I would certainly be open to discussion on potentially joining your firm. Would tomorrow morning be convenient for you?" You can see that your chances have improved by the way you introduce yourself.

One of the tools to obtaining your ideal position is being able to clearly express your goals to yourself and to others. You may need to write several résumés if you seek multiple types of positions, and perhaps, a unique résumé for each company. This, in turn, means doing some research before you write. You should know the scope of the job, the skills that a particular company is looking for, and a history of the position. Are the employers looking for a change or do they desire stability?

Gather information by talking with people who work at the company or know something about it, or who know people who know the company. You can look up company profiles in your public library's reference section. You can use the information you gather both in your résumé and in your cover letter. You can also use it during an interview to show you cared enough about the job to learn something about the company.

RÉSUMÉ LAYOUT .

Whatever the format, the résumé must be flawless. You should have no typos, misspelled words or grammatical mistakes. Your résumé should be attractive—use a high-quality laser and a good bond paper. White or cream colors are the standard and acceptable colors. As a minimum, your résumé must contain your particular personal information, including your name and address; the position you are applying for and your goals; and your qualifications, including past performance, skills, and applicability to the position. In highlighting prior experience, include the name of the company, employer or supervisor, the city in which it is located, the years you worked there (leave off months), and your title and responsibilities. If you have significant achievements, be sure to note them.

Try to avoid any discussion of salary because you may price yourself out of an interview or you may short-change yourself. Don't discuss your reasons for leaving previous jobs or similar matters that are best left for interviews. Also, don't include your references or mention that they are available—it is assumed that they will be supplied upon request. Eliminate extraneous personal information (e.g., marital status, age) as this information is no longer supposed to be relevant to your ability to be employed. Only include affiliations, hobbies and interests if they are pertinent to the job market.

The predominant discussion in your résumé should be your qualifications. These can be stated in any of the following ways:

CHRONOLOGICAL: This is by far the most common form of résumé. It lists a job-by-job explanation of your work experience. Chronological résumés are easy to organize and work well for people with many promotions to highlight. Construct a chronological résumé by listing all the relevant places you've worked during the last ten years. Leave out positions you held for less than a year or work experience irrelevant to your present goals. Normally, one should use a reverse-chronological ordering because it identifies most recent and relevant experience first, and readers have been known to be busy—sometimes to a point of reading early and then skimming the later data. If you use a forward chronology, the emphasis should show a constant pattern of growth.

FUNCTIONAL: Suppose you spend many years doing a variety of things for just a few companies. Maybe you raised a family and want to resume your career. A functional résumé may suit you best because it puts your skills ahead of your job history. Your goal is to highlight the attributes that are essential or useful in the job you'd like to get. In this format, accentuate the skills most pertinent to the desired position regardless of how current those skills are, and put toward the end those skills, even if recently acquired, which you would prefer to be less pertinent.

CHRONO-FUNCTIONAL: Here, as the name implies, you combine both formats to reach a targeted audience. You lead with a chronology of your work experience. In each job listing you show only the name of the company where you worked, its city and state (no street address), your title and the dates you worked there. Then, as in the functional format, list a job description of the types of work you have done across the multiple companies, and elaborate on your skills. This format is better than the functional format for job applicants who have the same types of duties and skills spread over several employers, and it avoids the redundancy of saying the same thing multiple times as would be the case in a chronological format.

REFERENCE LETTERS

A recently dated, well-written letter of reference from a former employer helps round out an application. You may also have available a letter of recommendation from someone with whom you've done some projects, such as a teacher or church member. Ideally, a fellow networker, particularly from your inner circle or friend network, will be happy to share a few good words about you. Such reference letters should be readily available at your interview, and should be volunteered if it appears that they would put you in a better posture. On the other hand, you don't want to "oversell" yourself, so don't prematurely present supportive information to the interviewer. He or she may think, that you think, you are under-qualified and are trying to use references in place of merit.

NETWORK LETTERS

Once you know you are ready and have the belief that you can get it, the next step will be to make it happen by getting networking into action. You must open the channels of communication. You have contacted the most likely sources that will let you know of job opportunities. Now you must follow through with your networkers, usually in person, but phone or correspondence is acceptable.

There's no telling where even a casual conversation can lead. For example, if the person you meet works in your field of interest, learn as much as possible about their environment. Is their business expanding or shrinking? Do they deal with companies that are doing well? Can they recommend avenues to help you further your goals?

One of your goals is to keep your network growing. Each time you meet a new person, ask for the names of other people who would be able to offer advice. Ask if your contacts know anyone employed in the same business whom they will call to supply a lead. This takes a bit of courage, but remember people do like to help others and are usually flattered when others seek their counsel.

With thought, sensitivity and preparation, networking becomes a natural way to build long-lasting productive relationships. Networking is an art, not a science. Yet, as a growing number of networkers recognize its potential, networking runs the risk of becoming routine and mechanical. A step-by-step, programmed approach to using networking techniques can destroy the aesthetics of the process and undermine its effectiveness. Networking should become a natural way to build productive relationships. There are six additional techniques you can rely on to improve your networking effectiveness:

1. Seek and use referrals. Cold calling may be the toughest approach, but will open an amazing number of doors. Be sure to say who referred you as a way to warm potential contacts and to a request a meeting. Spend some time on the phone if time or distance poses an inconvenience. If possible, go one step further by requesting that the person who referred you call or write a letter to introduce you. On the following page is a sample letter of introduction.

2. Research your contacts. It is important to know as much as you can about a potential contact. Your goal is threefold: to gather information, to cultivate additional contacts, and to be remembered when a future career opportunity develops. When you call or meet, there will be the ability to ask pertinent questions based on your knowledge of the person's background, expertise, and position. This information can be acquired from company publications and/or through business contacts.

What type of information would be pertinent to know about a potential contact? _____

_____

_____

_____

_____

_____

Date

Dear _____:

    Last week I met Jeannine Geiger at San Diego's Women In Business convention. Jeannine is from Sioux City, Iowa and is considering relocating to the San Diego area. When she described her banking skills, I thought of our meeting last week when you asked if I knew an aggressive human resource generalist with strong interpersonal skills and a good track record in recruiting.

    I was impressed with Jeannine's ability in developing a specialized recruiting and training program. Recently she developed a career articulation program for her bank, and she is responsible for recruiting within the technical and financial areas. She would like to build on her ability to coordinate closely with executives in designing and meeting new hiring needs. The bank has benefited from her sensitivity to managers' needs, creating good personality and skill matches, and she has been credited with the highest proportion of hiring and retraining statistics for our division this year.

    At this point Jeannine is exploring how to broaden her experience by developing some skills in compensation and benefits. She would like to move into a management role. I was impressed by her professionalism and forethought, and have no reservations about referring her to you. I gave her your name and phone number and told her to call you to talk about a position in your organization.

Your friend,

Signature

COMMENT: This letter applies the techniques of win-win networking—preparation, relationship building, personalizing each meeting, and follow-up. It also helps the applicant and the prospective employer by trying to match people to needs.

3. Prompt your contacts. Be specific in asking questions about information that may be of interest or help in achieving your goals. For instance, by knowing what you want and being able to express your goals, you may develop specific questions.

Whom do you admire and wish to become acquainted with?

_____ _____

_____ _____

_____ _____

_____ _____

_____ _____

_____

4. Seek and accept advice. Listen and accept advice with courtesy. Your goal is to develop a relationship that will be valuable over time. It is much better to ask for advice rather than to put someone on the "spot" by making them feel responsible for supplying what you want. For instance it would not be reasonable to ask someone to be responsible for finding you a new employer.

Reciprocity is the glue that keeps networks together. For example, a successful insurance broker fell on hard times when her company was bought out by another larger company. When times were good, she had been very generous by helping others. Now she was about to declare bankruptcy and was looking for a job. She confided her situation to her colleagues and asked them to keep their eyes and ears open for any career opportunities. By the end of the day, she was invited to go on an interview that ended with her acquiring a better position and increased salary compared to her last position.

5. Ask for names. Do you know anyone who could give me advice or would be willing to share their knowledge and give me ideas for future contacts? Develop a system to keep track of contacts. Keep your system organized so that it can become a valuable tool. Don't just put all those business cards in a shoe box! Consider a data base management package if you have a computer. Consider a Rolodex that is organized by profession rather than alphabetical in case you forget someone's name. There are other methods as well. How would you organize your system of contacts?

6. Follow-up. A critical, but frequently overlooked part of giving involves simply acknowledging advice, time referrals, lead or gifts from others. A note, phone call, or personal visit to express your appreciation—these are powerful tools in the networking adventure. If you don't follow-up within one week of each meeting, future opportunities may be lost. A progress report phone call a few weeks after the thank-you note will be helpful in maintaining your relationship. Remind your contact to call if he or she has any new ideas or information. A few weeks after the phone call you may send an article of interest or a cartoon. This follow-up will bring attention one more time. This subtle, yet effective approach provides a vehicle through which your contacts will be willing to help you.

How do you make a special effort to thank someone who does you a favor? _____

_____

_____

_____

How do you react when you aren't thanked for going out of your way for someone? _____

_____

_____

NETWORK CALLING

Once you have defined your goal and developed your network introduction, you can begin making network calls. This is difficult for experienced sales and marketing professionals, and even more so for people who have no experience. Networking to find a job puts everyone in a vulnerable situation. Still, telephone calls that can arrange network interviews are at the core of the networking process, and must be mastered. Here are some guidelines for success:

• Practice the delivery of your network introduction until you're sure you won't stumble. You should sound relaxed and confident.

• Plan the calls you are going to make each day. Make a list at the end of the day for the following day's calls, or do so early in the morning. As the sales slogan goes, "Plan your work and then work your plan." Before you deviate, take a moment to reflect on your goal. Will this deviation from your plan really help you towards your goal?

• Make the easiest calls first. Warm up a little before making the ones that may be especially important or difficult.

• If you are nervous about a call, try standing up and imagining the other person sitting. This will allow you to release nervous energy while you talk and give you a sense of physical advantage over the person you are calling.

• Frequently, you will talk to a secretary first. The secretary is the gatekeeper. Learn his/her name and use it in subsequent calls. Most people overlook secretaries, so they appreciate anyone who is genuinely interested in them. A secretary who likes you can be a great help. The reverse is also true. Here's an example of how a secretary can facilitate your networking: You call Ms. Jones and her secretary Sandy takes a message. Two days later, you call again. "Sandy? This is Anne Boe. We talked the other day. Your employer hasn't called me back. Is she out of town?" Sandy will most probably explain why her boss hasn't called back, try to put your call through, or at least suggest a good time to call. This is valuable information!

Since personal meetings are by far the most effective way to further your cause, and bluntly asking for a job doesn't work very well, you have to establish some rationale for the first meeting. The best one is to simply express your need for help. I recommend networking because people like to help people. Who can resist an opportunity to give someone else advice?

A request for help, properly expressed, usually works. Here's an example, "Good morning, Mr. Kelley, Ted Franklin gave me your name. I'm exploring career opportunities in electrical engineering here in Austin. Ted indicated you were very knowledgeable about the local situation. May I meet with you for fifteen minutes to discuss my objectives and get your advice?"

This approach inherently flatters Mr. Kelley, and avoids putting him on the spot. Once you are in the interview, you'll have an opportunity to demonstrate those qualities that will make him interested in you.

THE INTERVIEW

Interviews not only include the actual interview for prospective employment, but also the interview with the networker point of contact. It may be a person that you haven't met, but were referred to by another networker. The network interview is your opportunity to obtain general information about your job search, and obtain the names of additional networking contacts. You should consider any initial contact as an interview, and be prepared for the interviewer's desire to gain as much information as possible in as little time as possible. Most likely you'll begin by talking about yourself, often in a response to a question like, "Tell me a little bit about yourself." Your response is sometimes referred to as the "two minute drill," because it shouldn't take more than about two minutes. Write out your two minute drill, and then practice it while timing yourself. Your presentation for the first thirty seconds should include the following:

• Born and raised in . . . For some reason, people usually want to know this.

- Went to school at . . . Mention college, graduate school, special course work, but high school only if it has special relevance.
- Lived here since . . . If you're new to the area, briefly explain why. For example, "I was looking for a less frantic, less crowded environment," or "I prefer the pace of a big city."
- Spend the balance of the time on a brief career history. You should give enough information to show how you got where you are, but focus on your current job situation and how well you're doing, or how well you did while you were there.

Here are some more guidelines for conducting a successful interview:
- Plan the interview carefully. Prepare yourself with facts about the industry, the company, and the individual with whom you're meeting. Typically, the interview should begin with a restatement of the purpose for the meeting (your network rationale). You should then ask for the individual's opinions, and enter into a general discussion. At the end, always ask the individual for names of others you might contact. Finally, don't forget to express your thanks for the individual's time and assistance.
- Eliminate appearance as a reason for an unsuccessful interview. You should dress conservatively; comb your hair neatly; shine your shoes; use toothpaste and deodorant; use a pleasant smelling soap rather than an overpowering cologne or perfume. If you are a smoker, do without before the interview—it can give you an unpleasant odor, and may be perceived as a sign of nervousness.
- Be on time.
- Greet the secretary by name. Hopefully, you learned the name during your network call. If appropriate, use this opportunity to chat, build the relationship a little, and gather more information about the company or the person who has hiring power.
- Keep the interview to fifteen or twenty minutes unless the person you are meeting with extends it.
- If appropriate, make reference to the person who referred you.
- Show genuine interest in the individual, the responsibilities of his or her job, the problems, and the employee relationships.

- If appropriate, take notes—but always ask permission first.
- Don't offer a résumé unless you're asked. This presumes too much of asking for a job.
- If your new contact does ask for a résumé, request the names of people to whom it will be routed so you can follow-up with them.
- Establish the right to contact the person again to share your progress and ask for additional information.
- Immediately after the interview, write down any pertinent information.

EFFECTIVE TELEPHONE INTERVIEWS

During a selection process, due to the fast-paced business climate, a potential employer may decide to pre-screen a potential candidate through a short telephone interview. When you interview by telephone, you don't have the visual clues that so often help you to remember individuals and differentiate them from one another. All you have in a telephone interview is voice. Therefore, it is critical to take good notes.

At first, the telephone interview may seem impersonal. Once you try it, you will find yourself more at ease. Through careful planning and awareness you can create better results. Be aware that you will be evaluated on the following:

- Voice quality and language: You will want to be particular about your articulation, accent, vocabulary and grammar, speed, tone, the use of filler words (such as "um," "you know" or "okay") and volume level.
- Personality: Do you project a pleasant personality over the phone? Do project a smile and enthusiasm? Do you express self-confidence and a positive tone?
- Clear and concise communication: Note how clearly you describe activities, behavior, situation, physical objects and/or feelings. Are you able to convey information in a concise, easy-to-follow manner?

• Effective Listening: Do you pick up on what he or she is saying? Do you need to ask the same question to be repeated? You will be expected to pick up information quickly and accurately by just listening.

• Assertiveness: Do you probe to learn more about the position? Are you asking appropriate questions? Do you ask for a time to interview?

Be prepared to be questioned or evaluated upon your skills, background, experience and job expectation. Also, be prepared to gather as much information as possible about the position—you want to ensure that you'll be happy if you accept an offer. Don't depend on your memory. Write down where the job is located, company profile, job description, salary, and working environment. Since you likely will interview at several locations, you want to be able to compare the pros and cons of each.

THANKING PEOPLE

One important rule of networking—and of a successful job search as well—is remembering to thank people for their help. You should always send a written note of thanks to anyone who's been kind enough to spend time helping you with your search:

> Thanks for the Interview Referral
> I want to thank you for meeting with me to discuss my career transition. Your observations were interesting and useful. I also appreciate the referral you gave me. I will contact them soon. I would like to contact you again in a few weeks to discuss my progress.
>
> Thank you again. I appreciate your cooperation.

WHEN YOU SUCCEED

When you do land a job, don't suddenly abandon your network. To the contrary, you should review your relationships with the various members, and if appropriate, inform them of your success. You should revise your weekly networking goals downward, but not all the way to zero. In these uncertain times, everyone needs to maintain a strong network. By setting and meeting modest goals, you'll continue to nourish your network, and it will be there when you need it.

GET READY!

The next six pages were borrowed from the best job search books on the market, *Get Ready! Get Set! Get Hired!* Pages 143-145 were taken from the *Get Ready! Get Set! Get Hired!* textbook with the permission of the authors, Drs. Dahk and Jan Knox. Pages 143 and 144 are examples of functional and chronological résumés, respectively. On page 145, you will find the Fifteen Commandments of Professional Growth—great tips for any professional.

Plus, on pages 146-148, taken from the accompanying workbook, are resource forms that you can use to prepare for networking, company research, and job interviews. You will find these to be invaluable tools for professional growth and job search.

Good luck!

JACK L. SPRATT
202 Logan Lane
San Diego, CA 92154   (619) 575-0000

OBJECTIVE: To secure a position in Computer Systems Operations.

QUALIFICATIONS: Education, training and experience in:

Streamlined Software Systems	Wrote Software Manuals
Developed Software Products	Conducted Training Programs
Supervised Computer Projects	Delivered Training Overviews
Conducted Testing Analysis	Conducted Software Evaluations
Created Computer Forms	Supervised Quality Assurance
Automated Reporting Systems	Managed Electronics Procedures
Coordinated Configuration Management	Effected Program Savings
Controlled Operational Intelligence	Simplified Hardware Systems
Evaluated Tactical Software	Conducted Electronics Activities

EDUCATION: MS, Computer Science - West Coast University
                        MBA, Computer Information Systems - National University
                        BBA, Computer Information Systems - National University

EMPLOYMENT HISTORY:

General Dynamics Convair Division (1982 - 1990)
San Diego, California

Management:
Supervised configuration management procedures, manual rewrite, development of software manuals, and an engineering practices manual. Provided supervisory expertise for computer management services. Automated and managed a change status reporting system for product preparation and distribution.

Project Design:
Established and developed computer management system for automatic test equipment; developed cost saving forms, procedures and reporting systems. Automated parts shortage tracking to save considerable time and money. Created a standardized configuration status accounting report and formatting.

Writing:
Developed forms which resulted in a thirty-three percent (33%) reduction in paper usage. Wrote configuration management software development manual and an engineering practices manual. Streamlined formal reporting process.

Training:
Conducted monthly training overview and indoctrination for newly hired engineers; instructed usage of automatic test equipment design software system. Instructed computer software applications such as data bases, word processing, and spreadsheets.

United States Navy
San Diego, California
Senior Chief Aviation Electronics Technician

Duties:
Software configuration control management; tactical software test and supervisory evaluation; operational airborne early warning electronic warfare intelligence supervision; maintenance and quality assurance handling.

KEVIN BEAN
505 NORTH MOLLISON
EL CAJON, CA 92021
(619) 440-0000

OBJECTIVE: To secure a position as a LAN Support Specialist.

QUALIFICATIONS: Over 15 years experience.

PC DOS/Applications   Data Systems Tech.
PC Repair   Communications Tech.
Systems Configuration   Field/Customer Service
Testing/Evaluation   Troubleshooting
Microwave/uhf/vhf   Installations
Network Analysis   System Integration

EDUCATION: Grossmont College - Local Area Network Support
                           Specialist Certificate

                           Cubic Defense Systems - TACTS/ACMI Certificate

                           Apple Computer training Center - Apple Level 1 Repair Certificate

                           U.S. Navy - Data Systems Technician Certificate

EMPLOYMENT HISTORY:

CUBIC DEFENSE SYSTEMS, INC. San Diego, CA. **ASSOC. ENGINEER (3 YRS.) 1988 - 1991**
Assisted with system design and engineering. Development, testing/evaluation, implementation and installation of (80286) microprocessor based high speed data system. Microwave datalink.

GATEWAY COMPUTER, INC. San Diego, CA. **TECHNICIAN (1 YR.) 1987 - 1988**
Performed setup, test/evaluation and installation of PC hardware.

UNITED STATES NAVY DATA SYSTEMS/RADAR TECHNICIAN (8 YRS.) 1980 - 1987
Performed trouble-shooting and repair to the component level: Electronic Digital Computer Systems, Digital Display Systems and interfacing systems. Trained and supervised personnel.

K.G. SIGHT & SOUND Chula Vista, CA. **OWNER/OPERATOR (2 YRS.) 1978 - 1980**
Engineered, documented, sold, installed, and maintained Audio, Video, Satellite and Lighting systems.

STOPPER SOUND, INC. San Diego, CA. **FIELD SRV. MGR. (2 YRS.) 1976 - 1978**
Designed and prepared engineering drawings and specifications. Negotiated sales. Installed systems and instructed users on system operations. Implemented corrective/preventative maintenance.

The Fifteen Commandments Of Professional Growth

1. Thou shalt have a sense of humor and be able to laugh at yourself when you make mistakes or errors.

2. Thou shalt be responsible and accountable for your own actions, decisions and behavior; never pass the blame.

3. Thou shalt go the extra inch, mile or light year that it takes to become successful and your own person.

4. Thou shalt take chances, risks and gambles or you will never realize any appreciable gain or growth.

5. Thou shalt be a proactive networker with high visibility.

6. Thou shalt communicate effectively by listening to others, concentrating on facts, being receptive to learning, and taking in bits of knowledge daily.

7. Thou shalt have spunk and determination; never quit before you've given something your best shot/effort.

8. Thou shalt plan, prepare, practice and professionally present yourself in order to achieve proper placement.

9. Thou shalt hone and polish your skills, competencies and talents, least you become ineffective and stale.

10. Thou shalt be a go-getter: be assertive, aggressive and above all else, ambitious. Remember, attitude rules!

11. Thou shalt work at what you love, love, love.

12. Thou shalt be confident, reliable and unconditionally cooperative and helpful to others. You must be humble and serve, before you can earn praise and exultation.

13. Thou shalt have no hidden agendas, anger or resentment; play your cards face up and accept outcomes gracefully.

14. Thou shalt be candid, honest, truthful, tactful, and diplomatic in all circumstances and under all existing conditions.

15. Thou shalt be kind, generous, courteous, compassionate, understanding, and patient. Be a valued friend!

NETWORKING RESOURCES FORM

1. Business and trade organizations:

_____ Telephone:_____
_____ Telephone:_____
_____ Telephone:_____

2. Family and friends:

_____ Telephone:_____
_____ Telephone:_____
_____ Telephone:_____

3. Past jobs:

_____ Telephone:_____
_____ Telephone:_____
_____ Telephone:_____

4. Schools and agencies:

_____ Telephone:_____
_____ Telephone:_____
_____ Telephone:_____

5. Clubs and community organizations:

_____ Telephone:_____
_____ Telephone:_____
_____ Telephone:_____

6. New influential contacts:

_____ Telephone:_____
_____ Telephone:_____
_____ Telephone:_____

COMPANY RESEARCH FORM

Name of Company: _____

Company Address: _____

_____

Company Telephone Number: _____

Product and Services: _____

_____

Person Contacted: _____

Person's Extension and Department: _____

Positions Discussed: _____

Salary Ranges: _____

Company Benefits: _____

_____

Training Opportunities: _____

_____

Names and Positions of Key People:

_____   _____

_____   _____

_____   _____

Company Comments: _____

_____

Other Information: _____

_____

Referral Data:

Name:_____

Phone Number:_____

Name:_____

Phone Number:_____

Name:_____

Phone Number:_____

Name:_____

Phone Number:_____

Name:_____

Phone Number:_____

PORTFOLIO CHECK OFF LIST

Do you have the following items in your portfolio ready for your next interview?

1. YES NO   Copies of your Personal Resumes

2. YES NO   Copies of your Personal Information Sheet

3. YES NO   Copies of your Personal Reference List

4. YES NO   Copies of your Professional Reference List

5. YES NO   Copies of your Cover Letter sent to Interviewer

6. YES NO   A copy of your Job Application

7. YES NO   A copy of your Interview Questions

8. YES NO   Your Daily Calendar or Schedule of Events

9. YES NO   Copies of your Letters of Recommendation

10. YES NO   Copies of your Letters of Reference

11. YES NO   Copies of your Professional Certificates

12. YES NO   Copies of your Educational Diplomas

13. YES NO   Copies of your College Transcripts

14. YES NO   Copies of your DD-214 (Military only)

15. YES NO   Copies of your Enlisted Evaluations or Officer Fitness Reports (Military only)

16. YES NO   Letters of Appreciation

17. YES NO   Five Thank You Cards

18. YES NO   Copies of your Drivers License and Social Security Card

5
MANAGING YOUR NETWORK

"Anything done haphazardly will show.
Take care of business and it will take care of you!"

One of the golden rules of business is, "If you can't manage yourself, how can you possibly expect to manage anything?" More simply put, treat your network as you treat your business. Management skills don't deal only with workers or with projects or with inventory. The management skills needed for networking are in constant need of attunement.

By being aware of your goals and your ability to control events, you can achieve the success level of your results. We will examine how you can start and organize and maintain your current network more efficiently by improving your contacts, time, presentation, and organization.

"The most important word in the English language,
if you want to be a success, can't be found in the dictionary.
It's 'Rolodex.'"

—HARVEY B. MACKAY

MANAGING YOUR CONTACTS

Assess, reevaluate, and let go . . . to make room for the new. Periodically reassess your network since your needs, priorities, values, and contacts may change. What is suitable or important now may not have been in the past. Be aware of the changes in your life and adapt your network accordingly. Whenever there is a change in your career, a new focus in your life, or a new project on the horizon, you should do a review of your network. Redesign your network to stay closely aligned with your goals and who you are. By doing this you will be keeping yourself renewed and revitalized both at work and at home.

WINNING IS IN THE CARDS

A critical aspect of networking is keeping your business card file and follow-up system organized and up to date. Constantly add new contacts, and at least once a year delete those that may no longer serve your purpose. An excellent method for doing this is to gather all your business cards and make a conscious choice of whether to keep each contact in your network.

When trying to decide to eliminate someone from your networking system, remember the following definition to determine if they are worthy to be in your net: "Networking is a win-win process which links us to others and enriches our professional and personal lives. Effective networkers are actively exchanging and contributing leads, advice, support, information or time to make networking a mutual success." This process of elimination will include business cards of anyone that you have no recollection, or with whom you have had no contact in the last two years. These cards should be discarded or stored in a "near extinct" file. Now that your network has been cleaned and refreshed, there should be a feeling of a clearer purpose in your network.

EXERCISE

The time you spend identifying your network contacts is an investment in your success and the success of others with whom you share your resources. Begin by laying out your cards and writing each person's name in the appropriate categories by analyzing if you would contact each one in the following situations:

For intimate relationship:

_____   _____
_____   _____
_____   _____
_____   _____
_____   _____
_____   _____

For close friendship:

_____   _____
_____   _____
_____   _____
_____   _____
_____   _____

As mentors:

_____   _____
_____   _____
_____   _____
_____   _____
_____   _____

As teachers:

_____   _____
_____   _____
_____   _____
_____   _____
_____   _____

To have fun:

_____   _____
_____   _____
_____   _____
_____   _____
_____   _____

For professional advice:

_____   _____
_____   _____
_____   _____
_____   _____
_____   _____

For professional contacts:

_____   _____
_____   _____
_____   _____
_____   _____
_____   _____

QUALITY OF CONNECTIONS

Take a moment now to reflect on the quality of your connections to other people. I'm sure that you have noticed in the previous exercise that some names can appear in several categories. This is because networks are multifaceted, so it is natural for names to appear in multiple categories. On the other hand, look at your network and see if the process reveals any gaps. These gaps should make you aware of your needs and goals. If you need another category or two for your specific needs, create the category. What you are doing here is tailoring your individual networking needs, and expressing your ability to control and grow your network.

If you are contemplating making a career change to become a politician, for example, you may find it extremely beneficial to add more politicians to your network. Another category may address a gap in close friends. If there was a gap in that category, you will want to nurture those people. For instance, if you became ill in the middle of the night, whom would you call to take you to the hospital? Build a network that can support your professional and personal needs. Keep your network a dynamic source of energy and results.

A BALANCED SYSTEM

Support works both ways—you need to give as well as receive. Support networks function on the principles of exchange. Ideally, help should move back and forth between the people you indicated on the above support system. In the most effective nets, nobody keeps score of what goes back and forth. But you should have a natural sense to keep it balanced because imbalance can make another feel used or reluctant to interchange with you. Maintaining your support net is an important activity. Don't ignore it, or it might not be there when you need it.

You may discover the same people are providing many kinds of support. This may be an indication that you are depending too much on certain people. These people may feel burdened or for whatever reason may someday not be there for you. It could be difficult to re-weave your net during challenging times. The exercise you completed of assigning names to types of situations should be used as a guide for you to know who will be there for support and where you need to develop more support.

The best method of finding others to fill in any gaps in your network is to look for ways that you can help others. Compare notes, resources, and contacts with colleagues and peers. Being a resource is valuable to others, and thereby, increases your net worth.

SPECIAL PEOPLE IN YOUR NETWORK

Of all the people on the above list, write the names of the five people you most admire because of their personal and/or professional accomplishments. Also note why they were selected:

1. _____
because: _____

2. _____
because: _____

3. _____
because: _____

4. _____
because: _____

5. _____
because: _____

List any further comments, observations, insights, or revelations about your current network.

_____
_____
_____
_____
_____
_____
_____
_____
_____
_____
_____

SKILL BUILDER

Also, every day, mark down at least two business contacts with whom you will send a "Thank you" note along with your business card. If you can't send a note, at least make a phone call. Thank at least two friends every week. This is a sure method of keeping your personal and professional network alive and active.

DAILY NETWORKING PLAN

CONTACT NAMES

MONDAY   _____
TUESDAY   _____
WEDNESDAY   _____
THURSDAY   _____
FRIDAY   _____
SATURDAY   _____
SUNDAY   _____

THANK YOUs   _____
                _____

IMPROVING UPON YOUR WORK NETWORK

What people want from their job is changing. In the past, money, status, and prestige were the most important rewards. Today we certainly have not rejected the external trapping of success, but we want more. Most will agree that they want to work in a place where they feel respected as a person. They want to feel pride in their work and in what their company does. Large majorities want a company where they can be involved in the company's success. To accomplish self-worth, employees need to make personal connections with others to coordinate their efforts.

The success of a company can depend on networking. It's a win-win situation. Everyone in the company needs to be aligned with the company's mission and goals. The result is synergy, the combined action of the group that causes results greater than what anyone in the group is capable. Synergy develops when you know where the company stands, where it is going, where you stand within it, and how your own work connects to the company's goals.

EXERCISE

If you are feeling that you need to become more active in your company, do a comprehensive study of how your company really works. Begin by interviewing people, ask many questions, go to meetings, and move around. Like a good detective, you will discover why a company does the things it does, how procedures were developed, and what they mean. You may find the results of others who have recommended changes. It is important for you to know your company before formally proposing something new; especially to know if recommendations for changes are welcomed.

After completing the above exercise, you may know that a network exists but have arrived at the conclusion that you may not be using the network properly to enhance your personal or professional goals. Everyone can find it beneficial to advance their career by actively participating in the network of people who pass information about the organization's plans, decisions, actions, and benefits.

Before you start, you will need to know who reports to whom. How do the lines of communication work? For example, do you have a formal organization chart of your company. If not, you may want to design one for your organization.

IMPROVING YOUR PERSONAL NETWORK

As a society, we have isolated ourselves in many ways and often do not even know our neighbors. The cautionary words we heard as children, "Don't talk to strangers," can be adapted to be included in our behavior even though we are adults. But we don't have to isolate ourselves from the pleasurable experience of communicating with the people around us.

You don't have to go places to network; but as long as you are there you may as well engage in some pleasant conversation. By doing this you will be open to whatever may come your way. Perhaps you could make a business deal, find a new friend, or be introduced to another person.

New encounters can occur in elevators, grocery store lines, reception areas, restaurants, or any social or public place. You can approach others in a natural easy way. A good approach is a smile that acts as a great icebreaker. This should be a genuine, from the heart smile—the universal language. Smiles are welcoming and reassuring to others. When you smile at a person, they don't feel rejection. If a person responds to your smile, simply be friendly and don't force people to talk. Reach out to these people in a comfortable and gracious way.

Have several conversation generators in mind. Practice with a statement or question that is simple and that puts people at ease. Perhaps you have something in common. You can use a statement about the event, food, location, or size of crowd. Never start with a question that puts the other person on the defensive, or requires them to respond with factual matter. If the other person feels they could get the wrong answer, they will stifle further conversation for fear of embarrassing themselves. Your intention is to create a medium for information exchange, so you must get the other person to open up.

Obviously, you should use some caution in certain situations or locations of town. Could it hurt to strike up a conversation with the saleslady in a store? Certainly not. You just may find that she is a neighbor or a friend of a friend.

To help you remember people, be attentive and sincerely interested in what they are saying. Also, notice details by placing your full attention on every word and expression of the person with whom you are conversing. Introduce yourself to whoever you are speaking with if they appear to be trying to remember your name. You may save them some embarrassment and they will be more at ease knowing you've done them a favor.

"I've been on a calendar,
but I've never been on time."
—MARILYN MONROE

TAKE TIME TO MANAGE TIME

Time—it keeps ticking away. The seconds, the minutes, the hours, the days, the weeks, the months, the years—where do they all go? But wait just a minute! Who's in charge here, after all? Does time guide you or do you have control over your time? You have the choice to be a prisoner of time or the master of it.

Like most, you feel as if the merry-go-round is moving swiftly and your time is slipping away. Well, it's time to STOP! First, keep track for one week of how you spend every hour. Just jot down brief notes as you go through the day. At the end of the week take an inventory and divide your activities into categories: sleeping, eating, loafing, driving, working, recreation, and other activities. Then, being honest with yourself, determine whether you are spending an adequate amount of time working on those projects that have the greatest value toward your specific goals. If you are not devoting enough time toward your goals, then changes must be made.

EXERCISE

Review your activities and see what you enjoy doing the most. How many hours did you spend toward achieving your goal? How many hours are spent rejuvenating? How many hours are used strictly to support somebody else's needs? Make an hourly log from 8:00 A.M. to 8:00 P.M. for each of the seven weekdays. That's twelve hours a day, for a total of eighty-four hours a week. Your entry should be generalized into the predominate function for that hour, such as work, entertainment, relaxation, networking, and pursuit of your goals. You get the idea. When the week is done, total the hours for each activity, then divide by eighty-four. This will give you the percentage of time that you devote to each activity. Then, examine your percentages. Are you satisfied with the amount of time that you allocate to your own growth, or is the bulk of your time spent elsewhere? Are you wasting time in the evenings when you could be planning or accomplishing your networking activities? Make the necessary adjustments, and do this exercise again afterward. Then notice the difference and know that you are a time manager, not a time waster.

DAILY TIME MANAGEMENT

You probably realize more than ever, now, that each day is a new opportunity filled with a certain number of hours. If you find yourself not having enough time in the day to accomplish everything that is important, you will benefit from several practical time-management ideas. Each will help you be more professional and accomplish more in the time you have. It is important to develop a system for daily time management. Try this system for at least a month and see if you can see any positive changes in your time management. Each evening—you decide the time—list six items that you feel need to be attended to tomorrow. On the other side of the vertical line, next to each item, describe the benefit to be gained toward your goals by taking care of that item. Once you have clearly listed the benefit of each item, it becomes easy to change and set priorities. With this type of system you will be attending to your work according to benefits rather than taking care of items haphazardly. Do your sample here, and then implement it nightly.

IMPORTANT THINGS TO DO   BENEFITS

1. _____   _____

   _____   _____

2. _____   _____

   _____   _____

3. _____   _____

   _____   _____

4. _____   _____

   _____   _____

5. _____   _____

   _____   _____

6. _____   _____

   _____   _____

THE DAY PLANNER SYSTEM

Networkers know that their time is a valuable commodity and having a day planner system is an investment worth a fortune. A day planner system is a schedule and diary combination that becomes the central point for all notes, reminders, schedules, address book, business card file, and so forth.

If you don't have a day planner, go to a stationery or office supply store to see what types of day planners are available. Many planners have several different types of inserts, (such as things to do lists, travel plans, and so forth) that are available to customize to your needs or requirements. The best thing about having a day planner system is that you will inject action into every day of your life. As the days pass and your accomplishments become more numerous, your excitement level will rise.

Once you get in the habit of keeping your day planner every day, you will discover you have more enthusiasm in your actions, and this naturally leads to a dramatic increase in your productivity.

Computers are also a great tool to keep records—names, addresses, and phone numbers; follow-up information and what date to follow-up; and to categorize events, clubs, and other activities. Try my IBM compatible software package, *Get Ahead*, for tracking and nurturing your network every day.

KISS . . . KEEP IT SHORT AND SIMPLE

Make short and simple listings of all activities no matter if they are productive or non-productive. Detailed information is not necessary. As you add items for each hour, you will gain a great sense of satisfaction. At the end of the day you may be motivated to do just one more thing. If your day has not been very productive, you will be motivated to do better the next day.

☑ BOE'S GUIDE #37: Know where you are going so you can map your route. People often charge ahead without clearly knowing what they want to accomplish—their specific goals. They may find themselves working on what they were asked to do, going from task to task without a sense of overall purpose. Rather than blindly driving through life, it makes sense to begin by knowing where you are going before you map your route.

Setting objectives is the logical first important step in achieving effective time management. It is difficult to know how to spend your time if you don't know what you're trying to accomplish. Different activities lead to different results. You will gain and maintain strong support from management in your organization if you define your objectives clearly. These objectives should be stated in terms of purpose, benefits, and results to be obtained. Make sure your objectives are realistic and achievable. Think of your own goals, visions, and dreams and how you might make a difference in your job. One way to do that is to think about what change would result if it weren't for your contributions. Then envision the change that can occur through your efforts.

Focus on the total picture. Write out each step that needs to be done and the desired result, and these objectives will become realistic and achievable. Begin by making each of your objectives a specific project. A project can have an identifiable beginning and end. You can outline all the activities that must be accomplished to complete the project. The key to achieving both short-term and long-term objectives is to break them into smaller, more feasible projects. This helps you decide what to start doing now, and how to define the scheduled time. Don't set objectives and then miss getting started.

☑ BOE'S GUIDE #38: Set priorities: do what is important and let the rest go. It is necessary to focus your time and energy in those areas where they will have the most benefit. It takes talent to limit distractions and to avoid irrelevancies. You realize that it is not possible to do everything at once, so don't even try. Priorities begin with your objectives. Through networking you will know the most important objective to be accomplished for your organization. The most important objective will determine your highest priority projects and activities. Recognize activities that are meaningless or don't contribute to your goals and let them go.

Analyzing priorities involves consideration of two factors:
- Importance. The more important an objective, the more important the projects and activities related to it.
- Time factor. The time factor is the period related to the objective, project, and activities. Some things are more urgent than others.

In setting priorities, we must consider both time and importance factors because both are important when we must operate in an urgent situation or crisis. Something must be done, and typically it must be done immediately. The urgent or emergency crisis often develops because of neglect or improper preparation. People have a way to render themselves powerless because they cannot see the things that have to be done and put them into a logical order of priority. In an urgent situation, they tend to run around in circles in a panic and get less done than they could have in a routine situation.

Often, it is more tempting to respond to the urgency of something rather than to its importance. At one time, for example, there may have been plenty of time for action on a particular project. Now, however, there is a deadline and the project may have become a crisis. Many important tasks that are put off or unreasonably delayed finally get attention because they have become urgent. Be careful not to put off important matters until they become emergencies.

☑BOE'S GUIDE #39: Plan your time and activities. Planning might be defined as setting objectives and mapping out the activities necessary to achieve objectives. Managers, to be well organized and in control, must plan both activities and time. Scheduling is another word for planning time. When scheduling, you must think about how much time different activities will take, how much lead time is required for activities, dependencies of one activity on the completion of one or more other activities, and how to schedule things so that they can be accomplished in a realistic sequence toward the overall deadline. Furthermore, the manager must build in contingencies both for the slip in schedule of some items, and for the identification of alternate efforts that can be accomplished to avoid project stagnation.

One of the best ways to plan your time is to separate your objectives and projects into weekly plans, and then make daily "to do" lists. I recommend a weekly plan because a week has a natural beginning and a natural ending, as is the case for any good planning period. Also, there is greater flexibility in planning five days than in planning one day. Most people find that a week is well within the "time horizon" that future period in which you formulate work activities. The weekly activities must be planned before the week starts—otherwise, valuable time can be wasted on Monday morning waiting for the plan to be stated.

The key to successful weekly and daily planning is to be realistic about how long things will take. Generally, people are too optimistic about how much can be accomplished in a given period. When reasonable estimates are made, weekly and daily activities can be scheduled more accurately. Be sure to schedule time to handle unexpected events: they definitely will occur. Leaving flexible time in your schedule will not solve all your time problems, but it often eliminates time crunches and eleventh-hour crisis management.

For example, if you are planning a career change, plan it well in advance and treat it as a project. Think of all the activities that must be accomplished during the evaluation and write them down in a logical sequence. Estimate the duration of each activity and its appropriate lead time. Now you are ready to schedule these activities into your future weeks and days. By leaving yourself sufficient lead time, you will be able to handle any unexpected emergencies or crises that temporarily may throw you off schedule.

☑ BOE'S GUIDE #40: Get respect with presentations that are meaningful. If you have a presentation to make, follow the same basic planning and scheduling principles. Plan the meeting well in advance. Often, you have to plan several weeks in advance to find an available time for everyone who needs to attend. Identify an agenda and schedule all the activities necessary to prepare for the meeting, such as lodging or meal arrangements. Consider materials that should be sent to meeting participants in advance. Think about the graphs, charts, tables, and other visual effects that may be needed for the meeting. Don't wait until the last minute to develop them. Work that is done in a "fire fighting" mode is typically not done as well or as professionally as it would have been if it had not been put off until the last minute.

"Take what you can use and let the rest go by."
—KEN KESEY

☑ BOE'S GUIDE #41: Get on the A-I-R-Wave! Because of the nature of their job, managers and executives can become inundated with paperwork. Day after day, there are reports to read and letters to read and write. There are contracts to prepare and forms to complete. Then, there is their regular work.

If you're not careful, you can become so bogged down in paperwork that fire fighting becomes the normal response. Important tasks have been delayed, and it is the urgency of their deadlines that finally forces them to the top of the pile. There are no easy ways to avoid paperwork, unless, of course, the business world finally decides to adopt a paperless, computerized automated system. In the interim, there are several practical approaches that can help for paperwork.

Analyze your paperwork. Keep a record of the types of paperwork you receive and develop on a regular basis. You will find that it is not just a big undefined mess. You will find that it is fairly identifiable and predictable. Set aside time every day to tackle your paperwork. This way, the depth of papers in your "in basket" won't get too large, and you will never get more than a day behind. I know of a few people who handle paperwork as it is received, thereby not having a need for an in-basket. The detriment to this approach is that there must, then, be some other activity that is being interrupted.

The key to completing your paperwork is to initially handle it and subsequently take action to further its completion. A good first step is to take the time to sort your paperwork. Consider using the A-I-R-Wave technique to sort your incoming work:

A — Action
I — Information
R — Reading
W— Wastebasket

The "A" items are those that require a specific action on your part. As you review these materials, write in a corner the date on which the item was received, the date action should be initiated, and the date that all work should be started and completed. Ultimately, you will want to file these chronologically according to start date, and then once started, according to completion date. Every day, be sure to review each piece to ensure that you are on schedule. The items you place in your "I" file are those that inform you about day-to-day activities. They require no action on your part. They must be read now. Your "R" file is for newsletters, professional or trade journals, and industry reports. They are not reading materials that relate to your day-to-day work activities. These items have long-range impact; they relate to professional growth and to greater industry knowledge. The "W" symbolizes materials that are left over. Throw these in the air and wave good-bye to them as they land in your circular file (wastebasket). A good system will always leave time for networking!

TICKLERS ARE NOT LAUGHERS

Use tickler files. This is a good timesaving practice to keep track of important events and commitments. The most popular approach to organizing with tickler files is to use a calendar system. Organize thirty-one file folders, numbered one through thirty-one, for each day of the month. Then create twelve additional folders labeled January through December, and at least one additional file for the future year. As ticklers become appropriate for meetings, return phone calls, and important events, place the note into the appropriate month's folder. Just before the beginning of each month, remove that month's items and put each in its appropriate daily folder. Each day, check the appropriate day's folder for items to be responded to that day. Then, after completion, either discard the item, or file it in next year's folder or next month's folder if it is a recurring item. This way, you will not forget to take action on promised work, miss important meetings, fail to follow up on subordinates, or let any important event or activity fall through the cracks.

Avoid longhand. Writing things by hand, other than notes to yourself, not only wastes your time, but also the time of typists. Whether you are writing letters, memos, or reports, even if you have perfect penmanship, you will save time by using a dictating machine. If a dictating machine is not available, the next best option is dictating to a secretary. The pattern is the same for transcribing your materials. Transcribing well-dictated tapes is the fastest method and less error-prone; typing your longhand materials is the slowest and most risky methodology.

An alternative to dictation is the use of a word processing keyboard. If you do not have clerical assistance and have the availability of a word processor, learn to use it well. Knowing how to dictate effectively and how to type effectively are both good skills for the modern professional. You never know when your dictating machine or your word processor may break down. Why not be able to use both rather than having to rely on the longhand approach?

Color code your files. Use different color tabs on your file folders. Make all of your administrative files one color and use a different color for each type of file. You might also use the same color paper in the label holder on the front of the file drawer as the color used for the files inside. This reduces the probability that something will be filed improperly.

☑ BOE'S GUIDE #42: Being organized saves time. Unfortunately, even though you may have the greatest "Things to do" list in the world, you may never get to the first item on your list if you're disorganized. Having little to show for your efforts, frustration will be the norm at the end of the day.

Have you ever felt like getting a pile of papers off your desk by flinging them in the air, tossing them in the way a gourmet would toss a salad? Obviously if you do, it's time to improve your organization skills to suit our own personality and the task at hand.

As you plan your life and your workplace, resist the temptation of becoming too organized—it's an effectiveness killer. The main reason is that you will spend too much time organizing and not enough time living. Not only that, you will not get enough done because you are too busy organizing. Nevertheless, there are some good guidelines for organizing your life and your thoughts in the following paragraphs.

☑ BOE'S GUIDE #43: Those who possess the proper tools win. A tool is anything you use to help you achieve your goals. No matter what your goals or the activities you pursue, each of them involves the use of tools. For example, if you are a writer, your tools include a dictionary, a computer equipped with the proper software that provides a variety of fonts, a spell-checker, a thesaurus, a grammar checker, and the ablity to format camera ready pages with graphics. Of course, having these tools are convenient, professional, and they save time. Can a writer imagine going back to the days before Ben Franklin when books were written with quill and paper?

Make an effort to equip yourself with the best tools available. It has been said:

"The difference between wise men and fools
is found in their choice of tools!"

EXERCISE

Consider the environment in which you will be performing your work. Answer the following questions and if possible provide solutions:

Do I need a location that is quiet, private and comfortable to get
a task completed? _____

_____

_____

_____

_____

_____

_____

Is there enough proper seating, ventilation, and lighting?

_____

_____

_____

_____

_____

_____

Is there enough space to work and keep my essential tools?

_____

_____

_____

_____

_____

_____

Is there nonessential clutter in my workspace?

_____

_____

_____

_____

_____

_____

Do I have enough storage space for everything I need?

Are there recycling containers within easy access?

Would I be more efficient without a desk? For instance would I be more efficient if I had a lounge chair, clipboard, small writing table on caster, and file cabinets?

By answering these questions, you can arrive at your own solutions on choosing a style suitable for you and the work to be done. We all can understand that few of us do our best work with a heavily cluttered and disorganized workspace.

☑ Boe's Guide #44: Handle interruptions quickly and assertively, then get back to work. Telephone calls and unexpected visitors are the main sources of wasted time in virtually every public and private organization. Although an interruption forces you to stop what you are doing, it may involve the most important, most urgent project you are going to work on all day. It could be an emergency or crisis. These kinds of interruptions must occur. The others, however, are within your control to allow or to curtail.

The more frustrating interruptions are those telephone calls and drop-in visits that waste your time and reduce your effectiveness. You should attempt to eliminate or control these as much as possible. Remember that you want networkers to call you. So if you are able to do so, spend a little time on the telephone to keep your net alive and well. If it is an inconvenient interruption, however, cordially explain that you are in the middle of an event and that you would be very happy to return the call as soon as there is a better time for each of you. Your fellow networker will understand and thank-you, so make sure that you return the call. Keep these important points in mind when dealing with your interruptions:

• Socializing is an important part of developing good business relationships. You have to get to know other people, and they have to get to know you. The key is to control socializing, not to let it control you.

• You are constantly giving off signals to other people through the way you dress, groom yourself, and walk and talk. You are saying to other people, "Respect me, and respect my time," or "Don't respect me; don't respect my time." Your general demeanor must compel others to respect you and your time.

• People spend much time complaining about being interrupted. They rarely think about how much they may be interrupting other people. If interruptions are a major part of your situation, be sure to ask, "Am I contributing to the problem?"

Try these timesaving ideas for handling unexpected visitors:

• Stand up. If you remain seated you are extending an automatic invitation for the other person to sit down. If participants are standing, conversations tend not to last as long as they would if participants were sitting. Standing will also equalize a power relationship.

- Visit your networking contacts at their location. When you need to visit people who never seem to know when to quit talking it is easier to say, "I've got to go now" rather than "You've got to go now."
- Make your habits known right away. When they first visit, state that there will be times when you are busy and that you will be saying, "Well, I have to be getting back to work now." When they do visit, you may use the concluding phrase without offense.
- Set appointments with people you must meet. Tell them approximately how long you think it will take, offer a choice of times that would be convenient for you, and let them choose the one that is best for them. Appointments should also be used for routine business. You are probably being interrupted—and interrupting others—with a number of important but non-urgent matters. Just because something is important and needs to be discussed does not mean it needs to be discussed immediately. Keep lists of important items to discuss with the people with whom you interact regularly. The key is to set routine appointments to handle routine business, and not to treat everything important as if it were also urgent.

TIME SAVING IDEAS FOR TELEPHONE CALLS

Analyze your telephone calls. Find out who calls you, what they call about, what contributions the calls make to your work and the work of the caller, what time the calls occur, and the length of the calls. Analyze these data and you will discover many ways to reduce telephone time:

- Plan your calls. Before calling someone, write down the several points you wish to discuss so you are less likely to leave out something important. This way, you do not have to call back in a few minutes only to find that the person is on the telephone, has a visitor, or has left the office.
- Always state or ask for preferred call times. Let your secretary or other people know the best time to reach you by telephone. If someone answers your phone for you when you are away from the office, let him or her know when the caller should call

you back or when you will return phone calls. When you leave messages, suggest several times when you can return the call or when they can return the call to you. Work out the best arrangement. This will greatly reduce the probability that you will get involved in a game of telephone ping-pong.

• Always thank the person with whom you are talking. Networkers always leave a good impression.

Manage yourself and your time with the greatest of ease and see better accomplishments. You'll be less frantic, behind schedule, rushed and overwhelmed. If you manage your time, you will have a better likelihood of being able to do everything you desire. Enjoy all the hours of each day. Direct and design your actions rather than reacting to others. Good time management is not an accident. It takes an intense commitment and the development of good timesaving habits. Time management skills can be learned. Begin with your objectives, focus on the results you want to accomplish, and always consider the priority the importance and urgency of each activity. Plan your weeks and your days to accomplish as much as you can. If you practice timesaving techniques in performing every aspect of your duties, both you and your organization will benefit.

☑ BOE'S GUIDE #45: You have less than ten seconds to make a good impression! Don't wait for someone to magically appear who will introduce you to someone—this could take forever. Take initiative and introduce yourself. You need to have a planned and practiced self-introduction that is clear, interesting, and well delivered.

What you say about yourself should be tailored to the nature of the event or what you have in common with others who are attending. For example, if you are at a Parent Teacher's Association meeting, you may say, "Hi, I'm Jack Collins, father of Judy. She was the lead singer in the school holiday recital." As you can see, the introduction is tailored for the event and doesn't have to be long since a speech isn't necessary.

A tailored business introduction at a business related trade show may be as follows, "Hi, I'm Jenny Taylor, with Corporate

Trainers. My company provides guest speakers for major conventions in New Mexico. This is the first time I've attended a Chamber of Commerce Mixer. Is it your first time also?" As you can see, the self-introduction is different depending on the nature of the event. Your self-introduction may feel awkward at first, but with planning and practice, you will feel more at ease.

As your conversation progresses after the self-introduction, listen to your intuition. It will support your ability to operate, enjoy, and interact with people with greater comfort and ease. You will also experience less anxiety and stress as you learn to trust yourself and your inner sense of things. If you feel that the person you are networking with will be a valuable resource to enhance your goals, you will want to include him or her in your network. At this point a business card is usually exchanged. You may promptly send a letter or make a phone call to give a positive response and letting them know that you are appreciative and are willing to help others. This will remind the person of who you are as a resource, and your skills, talents, and abilities. Also, they know where you fit into their network.

YOUR TEN SECOND INTRODUCTION!

Communicating effectively, persuasively, and concisely is a skill that you can master with practice. You can survive and move ahead in business or in any other relationship if you can present your introduction swiftly and succinctly in ten seconds or less. Have your ten second introduction planned, organized, and memorized to quickly make an impression that will be remembered and generate a response.

Networkers understand that everyone must feel comfortable and effective when networking. A self-introduction should always fit the situation or nature of the event. For example, "Hi, my name is Anne Boe, and I'm into networking and career management. I'm here to do a presentation on the benefits of networking. Do you participate in many networking activities?"

EXERCISE

Write your ten second self-introduction. Say it aloud or practice saying it with a friend.

_____

_____

_____

_____

_____

_____

_____

_____

_____

_____

_____

ANOTHER EXERCISE

Describe an inventory of your people skills, talents and abilities.

_____

_____

_____

_____

_____

_____

_____

_____

_____

_____

_____

Identify major accomplishments in your life. How can you build upon them and create networking opportunities?

Now you have an appreciation for what you can do and what you must do. Your attitude is right, positive, and eager—now all that is left is to do it!

Personal Notes

6
NETWORKING FOR NETWORTHING

*"Good things will come to you when
you are doing the right things
and doing things right."*

By the time you read this, I hope you will agree that the acquisition of money is not a serious business; it is a game that you play. At first it may seem that it is a game that you play with forces outside of yourself—the economies of the marketplace. As you proceed, you discover it is actually a game you play with yourself. How you play the game affects the quality of your life and determines the extent to which you can liberate yourself. To liberate yourself you have to review what it is you believe about abundance and finances so that you can fashion an appropriate game plan which will take you from struggle to flow, from skimpy to lush.

PROSPERITY QUEST

I believe that in life we are on a quest. We are here to understand ourselves, including our physical body, intellect, emotions, spirituality, sexuality, love, family, friends, and wealth. You have to have it—otherwise there isn't much left for making life worthwhile.

There are so many ways of becoming rich. Let us eliminate some of the obvious ones so that we can concentrate on those circumstances in which most of us find ourselves:

• Inheriting money. But if you were not born into a wealthy family, acquiring wealthy relatives is going to be very difficult for you to control. It could be impossible!

• Being adopted. You can become so valuable to your new adopted parents and affect their feelings so dramatically that they consider you a relative even though you are not.

• Marrying into money. What are the chances of finding someone you truly love with vast amounts of money?

• Stealing the money: The end result is possible for you but with it comes certain nasty implications. Also, you many discover that, once you had spent the first million, you did not get the freedom you expected.

• Winning the lottery: Most people don't believe that they can do that since the chances are remote.

• Finding money. You may find a purse on your seat at a restaurant. When you return it, the owner may insist upon giving you a financial reward. The chances aren't likely of finding huge sums of money.

• Often people will consider themselves to be above money and feel so godly or so intellectually superior that they don't need to waste time with the day-to-day realities of obtaining it. Usually these types of individuals expects the world to keep them sustained and they are often angry when the system does not recognize this uniqueness.

As you can see, the chances of the above happening are remote. Of course, there will always be someone who will protest the importance of money by saying, "What about Mother Theresa in India?" There is no denying that Mother Theresa is a wonderful person who helps the poor in India desperately in need of her services. She also is a business. She converts her compassion and enthusiasm into obtaining money for the needy.

The philosophy which teaches that poverty is a way of life makes it difficult for people to attract money. They think that somehow their lack of creativity and effort will be blessed at a later date. This is evident in the phrase, "The meek will inherit the earth." I think they are in for a rude awakening. What is important is the contribution of money as a positive energy that will make the world a better place to live.

"I don't know much about being a millionaire,
but I'd be darling at it!"
                                        —DOROTHY PARKER

☑ BOE'S GUIDE #46: Money is a form of perpetual energy. Money needs to be circulated in order to gather momentum. Money you can give away, use to empower others, use to make the world a better place, and use to make your stay on earth a meaningful experience. Don't be afraid to be paid what you are worth. This gives you value and others will be appreciative and feel that they are acquiring value.

☑ BOE'S GUIDE #47: Money is only one form of abundance. There is also the abundance of happiness, of love, of opportunity, of friendship. It is often true that a person who is lacking in money is also lacking in other forms of abundance. It's the various aspects of their feelings that cut them off from the supply.

When you do what you love, the necessary resources will follow. Those resources could be money, fame, prestige, position, power, or other forms. Sounds great—what more could a person want! But all these resources have the potential of being disastrous if not used properly. For instance, when actors or actresses acquire awaited fame, they may discover their personal life is no longer as private as in the past. They may find they cannot lead a normal private life. It may become necessary to avoid people and constantly hide behind sunglasses when they are in public. Earlier, they thought the world would be wonderful if they were famous. Once they received fame, it was a disappointment. Discover your money values now—then become rich and famous by your own definition.

"It's not what you have, it's how you use it."

WHAT IS MONEY?

Money, fame, prestige, position, and power are not bad by nature. It's how they are used that determines the good or bad aspects. These prosperity items can be valuable tools for obtaining meaningful goals. However, as goals themselves, they are nothing but distractions at best, addictions at worst. People pursue them, get them, and wonder why they are still not happy. They may decide to get more, thinking it will solve the problem. They set their sights higher, get more of the same thing that didn't make them happy in the first place, and they are still unhappy.

Have you heard others say, "I'd be so happy if I only had more money?" Yet when they get the money they are still not happy. Money is just paper—a means to keep score in the prosperity game. It's the proper use of money that makes a difference. We have heard of many wealthy people with fame and fortune who achieve happiness in life by giving a portion of their money to worthy people or causes. They feel that they must return something for the money they acquired. They have an attitude that there is no such reality as "something for nothing."

Then there are those who think they would reach the peak of happiness if they only had money. These people are always relying on someone or something outside of themselves to make them happy. For instance, they feel they are somehow incomplete without having a great deal of money. As I look at the smiles on faces of impoverished people, especially children of India, I realize that a poor person who is happy is in a better position than a rich person who is unhappy. What is your perspective on obtaining wealth?

IT'S ALL POSITIVE ENERGY

The work you do or the investments you make are a part of the overall energy. By dealing with abundance in terms of energy rather than specific dollar amounts, you open yourself up to receive infinite amounts, for there is no limit to energy. Since energy is an abstract concept to the mind, it is easy for the mind to accept.

By following the concepts on the next page, you will create the total energy of what you are—mind, body, and spirit. This is how you develop your game plan with all the pleasant qualities. The following are characteristics possessed by successful networkers who know that money problems are only attitude problems. A networker with the proper attitude will have a much better chance of getting what they need. Say aloud the following powerful affirmations and give one of your life examples:

AFFIRMATIONS

I see problems as challenges.

Challenges make me stronger.

Life is easier because I am goal oriented.

I complete a job quickly without any excuses.

I am making a habit of having positive thoughts.

I enjoy finding creative ways to get what I need.

I wake up each morning with renewed enthusiasm.

I deserve wealth, health, love, and happiness.

The above affirmations can be learned, but with practice you will be surprised about how much easier and more rewarding it is to be positive and optimistic about what you are doing in your daily life. It's a well-known principle that the best way to learn is to teach. Teaching these things to others will greatly expand your understanding. There is much truth in the ancient Chinese adage, "Give a man a fish and you feed him for a day. Teach a man to fish and you feed him for a lifetime." I encourage you to teach others to fish for themselves, to be self-reliant, to be independent instead of dependent, and to be masters of their own fate. It's one of the greatest gifts you can give anyone.

☑ BOE'S GUIDE #48: Face your fear, for there is much more for those who dare. We don't have a shortage of opportunity in America. We have a shortage of courage. Once you understand this concept, you'll never lack again. As an example, there was a man who lost his job at a car manufacturing plant because the company moved to Mexico. With most of the town going into a state of depression, he had the choice of staying and trying to make the best of the lack of job opportunities in the town, or to be courageous and move to another town where there would be more opportunities. He discovered that the library had out-of-state newspapers. He read of opportunities, pursued them, and found an excellent job in another state. His new employer even paid his moving costs. So you see, he didn't have to sit around and mope.

There are opportunities everywhere—to meet new people, to start new businesses, to increase your income, to be of service to others. Simply keep your eyes and ears open and be creative in finding solutions to life's challenges. You should always have the courage to act out your dreams. You are worth it!

☑ BOE'S GUIDE #49: To be successful, you must learn to be yourself. Success does not always come by following the crowd. One of our deepest fears is the fear of rejection. We seek acceptance by our peers. We want to be loved. We crave it.

Look around you. Do you see multitudes of people standing in lines waiting for someone to take care of them. Step out of line and form a new line—one with you at the head of it. It may take courage to step out of the line marked 'security' into the line marked 'risk.' Others, including your parents, will tell you to play it safe; your banker will tell you to put your money in a safe, low interest bank account. The average American is confused as to what is best, and usually ends up being paralyzed. The few who are brave may dabble in a thing or two, get burned and retreat. Have you ever thought there must be a better way? Dare to be different by following your heart.

"The best way to be different is to just be yourself."
                                                    —TONY BENNETT

PARADISE

Well, let me introduce you to paradise—a better way to live. You can create a brave new world that will resemble the paradise you have seen in your dreams. This paradise is filled with opportunity, abundance, and freedom. It exists all around you, though only a few are ever able to see it. In paradise, your success and happiness are not determined by inflation, the weather, the government, or anything else. Your future is totally determined by YOU. To be part of this paradise, you will need to change your ingrained attitudes. Then you can collect the rewards of a better life. The following is what you need to do:

- Show willingness and be open to consider changes.
- Develop new habits of awareness.
- Seek new habits of time management techniques.
- Develop an attitude which sparkles with positive feelings.
- Find reasons to add enthusiasm to what you do.

Paradise is a place where you will take care of yourself physically—eat right, get proper rest, and exercise. There will be plenty here to feed your mind with powerful positive messages of great ideas, messages of unbending faith, and messages of optimism and hope for a much brighter today and tomorrow. Let's charge ahead, learn about priorities, and get on with our exciting life. You are special. You are tremendous! You are endowed with special resources! You have no idea what treasures are within YOU!

It may take you a while to see your paradise, but it exists as surely as you can see the sun. You can choose the paradise you want to live in. It's time that you feel free. I must warn you—once you enter this paradise, your life will change and you will never want to come back to the old world you left behind. Why would a butterfly go back to its cocoon? On the following page are a few samples of old attitudes that can lead to positive new attitudes:

Change your old world attitude
   into paradise.
Change "I'm dependent upon others"
   into "I'm responsible for me."
Change "I need security"
   into "I'm excited to find opportunity."
Change "I need friends"
   into "I have many friends who appreciate me."
Change "I need love"
   into "I'm worthy of respect and love."
Change "I'm a victim"
   into "I'm a volunteer."
Change "I'm an employee"
   into "I'm a boss, regardless of who I work for."
Change "I'm sensitive, go easy on me"
   into "I'm precious—challenge me, let me grow."
Change "I'm afraid of changes"
   into "I make changes in spite of fear."

YOUR INSURANCE POLICY

You may be wondering how you can avoid being overcome by your old world programming. The main attribute which will help you to stay on the positive side of life or paradise is the way you "picture" yourself. This is the real key to your personality and behavior. When you change your self-image, you change your personality and your behavior. The self-image sets the boundaries of your accomplishments. It defines what you can and cannot do. When you develop an adequate, realistic self-image, you will find new capabilities, new talents and literally turn failure into success.

It has been proven that the subconscious mind cannot tell the difference between an "actual" experience and an experience imagined vividly and in detail. It usually requires a minimum of twenty-one days to affect any significant change in any habit or mental image of yourself. Therefore, realize that you gain the greatest benefit if you reserve your judgment for at least three weeks. During that time practice, practice, practice and the new changes will have a chance to become part of your life. Simply play your new role for twenty-one days and you will experience improvement and perhaps, like many of my seminar attendees, tremendous results! Everyone with a healthy self-image has the right to the acquisition of material things. By nature people are goal-striving beings. And because that's what you were made for, you are not happy unless you function as you were meant to function—as a goal pursuer and achiever. Thus, true success and true happiness not only go together but each enhances the other. Knowledge and a positive attitude may be your best start to find these answers. Mix in common sense and action and amaze yourself at what happens!

☑ BOE'S GUIDE #50: Opportunities are often disguised as problems. There will be times when you will be tempted to avoid change. You will be tempted to not rock the boat and do things the old way. Temptations to take the easy, comfortable way can be viewed as problems that can become opportunities in disguise. Sometimes all it takes is the knowledge that you can do something differently. You see, knowledge plus practice becomes experience. Experience over time breeds confidence. If you are confident, you won't be afraid to try something new and different. When you are confident, you let others know what you want, you get it, and the world is yours.

Here's an example of a retired man who wanted to do something more in his life and at the same time, gain extra income. He would read his small town daily newspaper. One day, while reading the paper, he noticed the headline, "Elderly town citizens have difficulty traveling throughout the city." He organized a number of his friends who had vans or station wagons and started a transportation company strictly for the elderly. He later added wheel chair access. The business continues to be a great success!

EXERCISE

Have you found any great opportunities within the last month?

_____

_____

_____

_____

Can you develop a plan of action to act upon these opportunities?

_____

_____

_____

_____

Where will you obtain knowledge and/or information concerning these opportunities? _____

_____

_____

_____

_____

List the people who share your enthusiasm about taking advantage of these opportunities:

_____   _____

_____   _____

_____   _____

_____   _____

_____   _____

Make an affirmation: I, (your name) _____
will not stop until I achieve (opportunity) _____

_____

_____

_____

_____

_____

My rewards for accomplishing and incorporating this opportunity in my life will be the following: _____

_____

_____

_____

_____

☑ BOE'S GUIDE #51: Until you know value, everything is worthless. You will need to determine what is of value to you. Once you know and understand what has value in your life, you will recognize what is needed to obtain more of what you want in your life.

Every day unaware people pass right by opportunities—caught up in their own problems. They are going to work in the salt mine where salt is plentiful and labor is cheap. They are content to settle for a meager salary. Did you know that the word "salary" is derived from the Latin word "salarium" which means salt? Long ago, when salt was a precious commodity, many Greek and Roman workers used to be paid in salt. Thus, our word salary.

I'm not saying that having a job is bad, or that a particular job is bad in relation to another; rather, it is a common occurrence in our society for people to be working at jobs that provide no satisfaction. Many jobs are a great way to gain experience, confidence and ability. But why settle for a low paying job when you can have maximum income or maximum happiness?

"What is money?
A man is a success if he
gets up in the morning
and goes to bed at night
and in between does what he wants to do."
—BOB DYLAN

YOUR WINNING PRESCRIPTION FOR SUCCESS

It is normal to reach a point in your life when there is a desire for wealth. Wishing will not bring wealth but desiring wealth with the proper state of mind will bring the right opportunities to you. All you need is persistence and the belief that nothing will stop you from reaching your goal. Be obsessed! The method to realize your desire for wealth in your life includes the following prescription for success. Place all this information where it can be viewed each day. Most importantly, pretend it's yours. Experience it as though you already have it. You already have wealth.

Write a clear concise statement of the reason you need a certain amount of wealth.

_____
_____
_____
_____
_____
_____
_____
_____
_____

What is your purpose for attaining this specific amount?

_____
_____
_____
_____
_____
_____
_____
_____
_____

Decide the time limit of when you will receive the wealth.

_____
_____
_____
_____

What can you give that will be beneficial for the acquisition of wealth? _____

_____
_____
_____
_____

Describe the plan for carrying out your desire and begin at once. Be involved and take action toward getting what you want— "Action for satisfaction."

In what ways will you be grateful for what you have?

_____

_____

_____

_____

How will you express your gratitude?

_____

_____

_____

_____

Finally, is this what you truly want? Will you have the love, commitment, desire, and perseverance to make it a continued success?

_____

_____

_____

_____

You may want to start doing these steps in order, and you may find that some of them happen all at once. For example, you may find yourself doing some steps simultaneously. If there is confusion or doubt, however, just separate them, and do them one at a time.

People throughout the world have used this formula for success. Of course, some things are easier to achieve than others, and some things may take a longer time to manifest. It depends on the nature of your chosen priority. Also, it may be of further help to know that these steps were used by Thomas A. Edison, who recommended them as being not only steps essential for the accumulation of money, but for the attainment of any goal. As you completed the above questions did you notice that you used sufficient imagination to enable you to see and to understand that accumulation of money cannot be left to chance, good fortune, and luck.

This process will work if you work it. If you review these steps and your life doesn't seem to be moving you toward your goal, take a look to see if you're omitting any steps. You may as well understand that you must find the truth for yourself by being true to the process.

"Insecurity is the result of trying to be secure."
                                              —ALAN WATTS

☑ BOE'S GUIDE #52: Networkers know the correlation between contribution and making money. Networkers are secure with money. They know that money is a tool to facilitate exchange—a form of creating (obtaining) what they want while helping someone else meet their goals. You will always be wealthy when you have an intense desire to contribute to the good of others. Your urge to donate your talents will be rewarded with prosperity. This is the universal law of action leading to reaction.

I believe that each of us really wants happiness, and to the extent that we aspire to wealth, we erroneously believe that money will make us happy. Happiness is a by-product of a meaningful life. We all recognize several examples of people who are financially secure but are not happy. That is not to say that money can't buy you many things that can make your life more pleasant. Like happiness, money is a side effect of a higher purpose.

The forces of nature want to be in balance. Love of money to the exclusion of everything else will cause you to become unbalanced. If you have your heart set on money, and place all your attention on making a fortune, you will find yourself lacking in other areas. You may make a fortune, but you most likely will find yourself excluding friends, loved ones, society, and social activities. You can become isolated, inhibited, and frustrated. It is not a good feeling to hunger for peace of mind, harmony, love, joy, or even perfect health.

What I'd like you to do now is list your current belief system about money:

What does money mean to you?

_____

_____

_____

_____

How much do you need as a minimum?

_____

_____

_____

What amount of money would make you feel that you don't need any more?

_____

_____

_____

_____

What would you do if you had all the money you desire?

_____

_____

_____

_____

_____

_____

AFFIRMATIONS

I am here to lead an abundant life, to be happy, radiant, and free.

I have all the money I need to lead a balanced happy, full, wonderful life.

There is no virtue in poverty. I am here to grow, spiritually, mentally, and materially.

I will surround myself in beauty and luxury.

Wealth is my friend. I will always have a surplus.

Every day my wealth is multiplying. I am advancing, growing, and moving forward financially.

I am prosperous; I am successful; I am wealthy.

I am a contributor.

WHO'S MINDING THE STORE?

Networking activities have to be tracked. Follow-up is crucial. Networking correlates with networthing! Networking is your key to financial and relationship success. I want you to begin to think of money as energy and something you need to keep circulating and drawing in. You will receive financial rewards as you strengthen your career success.

As you become more influential in building your network, you will automatically open up additional business opportunities. These opportunities will eventually lead to additional money and recognition. It is very important to keep your financial goals in mind along with your career and relationship goals. Ask yourself the following questions:

What part does money play in your career success?

_____

_____

_____

_____

_____

What does money represent to you in your life?

_____

_____

_____

_____

_____

How have your financial attitudes changed since your self-esteem has become stronger? _____

_____

_____

_____

_____

What are some additional ways to expand your financial base within your career? _____

_____

_____

_____

_____

☑ BOE'S GUIDE #53: Networkers know that there is a direct relationship between yourself, your confidence, and your financial well-being. Networkers are able to draw resources, people, and ideas to them because they believe they are worthy of tremendous business success. As you heal your self-worth issues, you will draw in better relationships, a healthier prospective to your career, and begin to see that you have a direct influence in creating your financial success. Networkers know they deserve the best in whatever way they choose to define it.

Money is a thought form. It is a symbol of energy and as such, has no real, intrinsic value. It is neither good nor bad, positive nor negative. Money is impartial. The person who wrote that "money

is the root of all evil" must not have had any! You can't make it
through life without it. Sometimes the love of money can cause
people to become greedy; but, it is fact that without money you
cannot be free. Poverty is restriction and, as such, is the great
injustice that you do not want to perpetrate upon yourself.

Many times you may know a principle but when you go to
apply it, something doesn't work quite right. For example, having
the knowledge isn't always enough. Timing can be a factor as well.
The rewards can be in the wisdom of how and when you apply the
knowledge. Consider this example: When Becky was thinking
about applying for a position as a graphic artist assistant, she knew
that the head of the division was expecting to win a big contract.
Had she applied during his time of anxiety, she may have been
discouraged. Instead, she waited until the contract was won before
applying for the position. She received the promotion by catching
him at a time when he was in a good frame of mind. Timing is of
the essence. You may have the right message, but be sure you pick
the right moment to let it be known. In other words, be sensitive
to other people's feelings and career situations.

☑ BOE'S GUIDE #54: It doesn't take money to make money. Many
have been programmed all their lives to believe that it takes money
to make money, so they don't even look! Lets concentrate on finding
opportunity. For example, if you feel your current position lacks
challenge, perhaps you should consider calling others to inquire
about opportunities. By accepting another job or putting into action
entrepreneurial ideas, you will have more opportunities to increase
your net worth which, in turn, will lead to increased earnings.

☑ BOE'S GUIDE #55: Those who live by the golden rule, get the
gold. You can solve your own money problems by learning to
solve another's problems. It may be a whole new way of looking
at the world, but it works!

If a business person doesn't solve your problems in a win-win
way, he's out of business. Business people are forced to do good
unto others, or they won't be "done good unto." Living the golden

rule is the most important and practical business principle that networkers need to live by. It's common sense that when you concentrate on solving other people's problems fairly, your reputation will spread. A solid reputation is as good as money in the bank. Besides money in the bank you will enjoy valued friendship, goodwill, and recognition.

☑ BOE'S GUIDE #56: Money is attracted to good ideas. Money always flows toward great opportunities. If you have a good idea, someone will recognize and like the idea. If you need money, you will find a wealthy person who would like to financially support your idea.

Remember, the greatest asset is yourself. What you are is more important than what you have. What's inside you is more important than what's outside of you. Your non-financial resources are more important than your financial resources. Yet, people will still yearn for the appearance of wealth fancy cars, cash in the bank, big houses, and vacations. These things are just the by-product of wealth, not wealth itself. Wealth is rated by knowledge, skill, and courage—not by wealth itself. So now you know that you are already wealthy. You are your own gold mine.

☑ BOE'S GUIDE #57: Sometimes people get stuck in neutral and just wait for the light to turn green. There are usually three common reasons that can make you paralyzed with inaction:

• Fear—When something is important to you there will be a strong desire to take action. Always feel you deserve freedom to make choices. Make the results of the goal stronger than the fear.

• Start-up—Don't wait for everything to be perfect before starting. Start with knowledge and education. Go to someone who is already successful at what you want to be doing, ask them for their advice and take action!

• Economy—There seems to always be something detrimental about the economy, so don't wait for it to improve. Take action now—it's the only way to take control of your life.

EXERCISE

Are there any reasons you have not completed a major goal in your life? _____

_____

_____

_____

_____

What can you do to make your goal achievable?

_____

_____

_____

_____

_____

☑ BOE'S GUIDE #58: There is no failure—only feedback. Many people do not attempt to make their dreams a reality because they are afraid of failure. By now, you should recognize nothing will be achieved if nothing is pursued. You most likely, have heard the phrase, "nothing ventured, nothing gained."

Can you imagine the world today without electricity, air conditioning, telecommunications, or other modern conveniences? Of course, we are grateful to the inventors who treated their multitudes of failures as feedback on ways of how not to do something! I feel that if you know what you want, have the belief you can get it, and obtain the knowledge and skills, there should be no limit to what you can do!

AFFIRMATIONS

I will always think positive thoughts.

I will associate with a network of positive and prosperous people.

I will practice my skills.

I will motivate myself by taking action toward my goals and by setting deadlines.

I will plan my work, and work my plan.

I will acquire knowledge from great and successful people.

I will aspire to be the best I can be.

I will assist others in achieving their dreams.

☑ BOE'S GUIDE #59: A successful networker will develop a routine of daily self-improvement. It will be up to you to establish a daily routine to fit your lifestyle. The following are some ideas of planning: Time spent:

	Daily	Weekly
Your Master Planner	_____	_____
Goal review and visualization	_____	_____
Organization and "to do" list	_____	_____
Exercise	_____	_____
Reading motivational books	_____	_____
Family, friends (spend time)	_____	_____
Attend network meetings	_____	_____

☑ BOE'S GUIDE #60: You can never be too organized. Do you ever feel you will never get your life together? Successful people always seem to have extra time to enjoy what they want to do. In my opinion, the major reason why successful people always seem so "together" is they set specific written goals with realistic deadlines. This sends a message to the subconscious mind to automatically sort through the confusing detail of life and only notice that which advances them toward their objectives and goals. Since they know what they want, when they want it, and how to get it, they don't have to waste time agonizing over every decision.

Did you know your conscious mind can effectively hold only five to ten thoughts at a time? If you don't want to feel overwhelmed, write down all the things you have to do. The next step will be to prioritize your activities according to importance or convenience. You'll be surprised how much less confusing it is once you get the list down on paper.

Also, remember that you should keep track of your progress on a regular basis. Take time to see if progress is being made and record your insights and experiences in a daily journal for review on a regular basis. After a few weeks of practice you will notice that you are becoming more serene, calm, and organized in a world that thrives on confusion and chaos.

EXERCISE

Do you feel there is unnecessary confusion and chaos in your life?

_____

_____

_____

_____

_____

How can you reduce or eliminate any confusion and chaos?

_____

_____

_____

_____

☑ BOE'S GUIDE #61: Learn to trust yourself. There are no failures or wrong answers, only feedback. Hopefully you are ready to take charge of your life, to stop being dependent, and to be the master of your own destiny. You will notice a new power—a new energy come into your life. It may not happen overnight, but you'll begin to notice that a new awareness is overtaking you. You will become more creative, happier, more confident, and more at peace. People will notice that you seem to exude a quiet power. That's what will happen when you learn to trust yourself.

AN INTERVIEW WITH MARY

While on a six-hour plane trip to the east coast, I happened to sit next to a woman who seemed to exude success. She was happy and filled with enthusiasm. She talked about her successful career as a real estate broker and the opportunity to buy a home on Cape Cod as a vacation home and investment.

I asked her if her life was always so positive. She said, "No. Only two years ago, I was ready to throw in the towel. It was depressing. I hope I never have to feel like that again. Today, I have a feeling of expectancy, as if good things are just around the corner—this sense that the things that I've been preparing for all my life are beginning to come together. I think there's a German word for it, Zeitgeist. The idea is that when a person takes responsibility for his or her life and chooses a path, certain unknown spiritual forces begin to erupt around them. My success started when I established a goal—one that I felt was realistic, attainable, and challenging, to buy at least one property a month for the next twelve months. After I knew what I wanted, I began telling others what I wanted, and one thing lead to another and here I am through a referral from a friend of a friend about this coastal property."

I couldn't help smiling as I listened to the rest of her story. "This hasn't been a piece of cake," Mary said. "It didn't happen overnight. I sometimes feel I've been on a surrealistic journey! This wasn't a dream though—this really happened. I was searching for a magical formula to make me happy. I discovered I had the key all along. I now have a whole new level to my life. I used to stay home, afraid to venture out into the world. Now I understand the risks. I'm confident that I can handle the surprises and take things in stride without falling to pieces. I've experienced the rewards of my hard work. Those rewards are what makes it exciting!"

I interrupted her. "Would you have learned these things without experiencing them?"

"No," she answered. "None of the information made sense to me until I also lived it. It's just like having your first baby. You can read every book on how to have a baby but until you experience it, nothing can compare to the real thing."

We both agreed that there are no secrets to wealth. Clear goals, common sense, and a commitment to action leads to experience and reward.

I told her I was writing a book concerning networking, and asked her what she thought prevents so many people from reaching their full potential. Mary said, "Fear holds a lot of people back. A person should put aside his or her fears and doubts and just do it. Don't let anyone talk you out of your dreams. Believe in yourself. Believe that you have a purpose on earth. Write down what you want, and say it to yourself every day. Then never give up. Don't let anyone discourage you!"

Mary continued, "Things became much better when I realized I could enjoy being myself. I could be well dressed, presenting a client at an escrow meeting, and an hour later be wearing shorts and tee shirt wrestling with my kids. I can be myself—a mother with two toddlers—and be successful at real estate at the same time."

"Do you feel wealthy?" I asked.

"Yes. In my own way," Mary answered. "I don't think I'll ever gauge my wealth in terms of material possessions. Of course, the positive side is that I have some valuable assets—an identity, a brain, and a plan. That's when I began to like myself!"

"There were times that I felt that I had bottomed out and couldn't see any way out of the bad times. Someone gave me a tape by Robert Schuller called, *Tough Times Never Last, But Tough People Do*. It inspired me to understand that it's not who's first but who crosses the finish line."

Mary continued, "About a year ago I was observing a marathon for handicapped children along Mission Bay in San Diego. As a small deformed boy jogged past the finish line, the crowd cheered. Then a hush came across the crowd as a lone teenage girl fell, got up and staggered back onto the track trying to reach the finish line. She was bruised and in obvious pain, but I could see the determination on her face. The doctors ran onto the track, concerned about her condition, but she waved them away, knowing that if they touched her, she would be disqualified from the race. The crowd was moved by this display of sheer willpower and shouted encouragement as she completed the final few yards. When she crossed the line, the crowd cheered more for her than for the boy who had finished first."

"It gave me chill bumps." Mary said, "That's how I feel about the challenges in my life. I know it took a long time and extra effort to build my business, but I'm going to cross the finish line! I'm sure you heard the saying, 'It's not important whether you win or lose, it's how you play the game.'"

"To be constantly striving is to be fully alive."

Personal Notes

7
NETWORKING
NOTABLES

"The networking community is filled with notable people.
Now it's your turn to become one!"

Every day I hear from other networkers about their excitement
and enthusiasm. They are filled with the desire to share information, and I am anxious to share my insights with them. For this
book, I thought, what better source of networking insight than
from networkers themselves! I asked a few "networking notables"
if they had any words of wisdom for you, the reader. The response
was overwhelming! In this chapter, it will be my pleasure to share
with you some of the thoughts of my wonderful business friends.

GOING TO REAL LIFE NETWORKERS FOR THE ANSWERS

It was quite an enlightening experience to have the privilege of
interviewing our selection of notable networkers who seem to have
it all . . . financial freedom, access to others who help them to get
what they want, satisfying relationships, and the ability to make their
dreams become a reality. These special notable networks are superachievers who know that networking is more than a "buzzword."
Networking made it possible to build the bridges that create an

expanded resource pool. Networking is one of the talents these superachievers have mastered. These people enjoy the exhilaration of being able to make their own choices and to break through the limits and barriers so that they can control their own lives. One thing that they will all agree upon is that without networking, this freedom wouldn't be possible. These networkers are the best and brightest stars. They know the importance of the following:

- taking action and making connections
- offering support and opening doors
- creating access and visibility
- coming from kindness, sincerity and compassion
- giving without expectation
- being willing to share
- having long-term win-win relationships
- enjoying their personal and professional lives
- seeing the connection between giving and career success

By following their examples, you can build a support base that connects you with qualified, confident, and competent people. These networkers know the value of having a resource bank which provides a referral and a promotional system. The payoff will be found in the opportunity to establish and maintain connections with stimulating people who aid you in opening new ideas, contacts, friendships, and ultimately business opportunities.

We realize that all the questions about successful networking cannot be answered by directly contacting networkers. However, we did get wonderful information from many networkers who are successful business professionals from all walks of life and who generously shared their stories and experiences. We interviewed the experts in their respective fields, whose success stories became oracles. Our main curiosity was whether their know-how could show us the way? These individuals show a large diversity that makes for a brilliant kaleidoscope of skills, experiences, and contributions that teach and inspire. Each defines success in their own terminology. Success for each is made up of a smorgasbord of any or all of the following elements: satisfying personal relationships,

fame, career and personal achievement, inner peace, wealth, inde-
pendence, and joy.

Many viewed their accomplishments as the natural outgrowth of
learning better ways for improving their life. They mentioned that
some of their life's learning experiences were painful and difficult,
but were important because they increase knowledge and broaden
their experience base. This ultimately brought them joy and stimu-
lation while adding beauty and wonderment to their life.

EXERCISE

How would you define success in your life? Satisfying personal
relationships? Variety ? Fun? Friends? Give an example for each
that you list.

_____   _____
_____   _____
_____   _____
_____   _____
_____   _____
_____   _____
_____   _____
_____   _____

The secret to their success is no secret. These people may not
be more intelligent or more talented than others; but they most
likely work "smarter not harder," are more driven, have more
vision, and welcome the challenge of setting high goals. Their
most apparent qualities include:

- showing their passion through nonstop compelling ambition
- having a passion for their job
- knowing their wants, needs, and desires
- liking the challenge of work
- feeling privileged to experience the feelings of satisfying
  relationships
- being intensely focused

- being extremely effective in what they do
- having their energy harnessed and concentrated
- having deeply rooted belief in themselves
- wanting to leave their mark
- having grand scale visionary thinking
- enjoy taking risks
- not minding the challenge of obstacles
- not allowing the word "can't" to be in their vocabulary
- possessing business savvy
- demonstrating that they are strong people and good with communication skills
- being zealous learners
- knowing that life is full, rich, and fun
- having high self-esteem and confidence
- having great sense of determination
- demonstrating an ability to make good decisions
- showing that they are good at self-care and self-nurturing
- having the ability to connect with others
- willing to ask for help

NETWORKING TIPS

1. Smiles are said to be the universal language. A smile is reassuring to the other person and makes you approachable. When two people smile it makes everyone feel good.

EXERCISE

Go ahead and smile and then frown. Did you notice that it is easier to smile? It takes a lot more muscles in your face to frown! If you ever catch yourself frowning, think of yourself turning upside down, to turn that frown into a smile!

2. Take initiative in meeting people. Warmly make your handshake from your heart as you look directly into one's eyes as you start your conversation. A friendly greeting such as this is hard to reject!

EXERCISE

Practice extending your hand (no dead fish handshakes allowed) and strike up a conversation with a friend.

3. Show interest in others. Ask meaningful questions without being too personal. You want to bring out the best in people by giving them a chance to shine as they talk about events or ideas important to them. Notice details about their lives and comment upon them. Everyone enjoys recognition of what they feel is important in their life.

EXERCISE

You have just been introduced to John Herald, who is the president of a local bank. What would be your first comment or question? _____

_____

_____

_____

_____

4. Make a conscientious effort to remember people's names and use them. It always makes a good impression on someone when you say their name. When you meet someone say their name, and if possible write something special about them on their business card or in your daily planner. When you communicate in the future, refer to that information.

EXERCISE

Do you remember the person's name that you last met? Did you exchange a business card? If you didn't write anything on his/her card, what would you write, to make you remember that person better? _____

_____

_____

AND NOW, A WORD FROM OUR NETWORKERS

I wanted input from my fellow networkers, so I asked. Naturally, my request did not go unanswered. I received a wide variety of answers to these two basic questions: "How has networking worked for you in your business and/or career?" and "How has networking contributed to your relationships and financial success?" Here are what other networkers feel. I won't repeat the questions for each answer.

How has networking worked for me in my business and/or career?

Seeing Anne's "Networking" presentation at the 1992 Council of Logistics Management Conference in San Antonio, really opened my eyes to how I was conducting myself in the business world. Her work dramatized the fact that networking, using Anne's approach, is an extremely valuable tool in today's world. Anyone not taking a serious look at this vital subject, and how it can absolutely change your life, is making a serious mistake. It is an entirely new "mindset," and it has changed my outlook and direction to everyday interpersonal activities. I thought so much of her work, that I wanted to share it with my cohorts. We had Anne in for a seminar with the Holiday Inn and the Rolling Meadows, IL Chamber of Commerce. She made such a major impression on everyone that they have invited her back for next year.

How has networking contributed to my relationships and financial success?

Networking and it's value has come to me in the form of opening my eyes to what's best for my company and me. I realize that no one person can accomplish everything they need to all by themselves. Working endless hours and trying to tackle major activities with even more hours is not the answer either. There is a gigantic wealth of cooperation existing in your community today, so take advantage of it. You can be a part of your community by learning the best networking methods available. Anne has made a science and an art out of these methods. You have to take the first step. That is to make the commitment to change! Anne's approach requires only that you learn the basics of interpersonal skills—those of sincerity, honesty, and integrity. If you want a friend you have to be a friend, and mean it! Make the commitment to "just do it" applies in the world of Nike and even more so in interpersonal skills.

Wynn Topley
Corporate Director of Distribution Systems
Pepsi-Cola General Bottlers, Inc.
Rolling Meadows, Illinois

Networking has made the difference between success and failure in my business. Without a keen sense of networking in marketing and public relations my ideas would go nowhere and certainly not to the right people.

Networking has helped me cultivate relationships and be on the cutting edge when big business deals have come to fruition. In my opinion, networking is the bridge that fills the gaps to help good business people get to the top.

Lynn Weller, Marketing Manager
Kennestone Hospital
Marietta, Georgia

Networking has continued to help me in both my business and career. Over the past fifteen years in the direct selling industry, networking has allowed me to assist many others to secure positions in the industry as well as helping me to locate and use "support resources" in the companies with which I've been associated. Using these support resources has made me more "sales efficient and cost effective."

Networking has absolutely contributed to my business relationships and directly to my financial success. Because of my dedication to networking, I'm considered a valuable "source" within the direct selling industry in terms of helping others with personnel, program, premium, training, and ethnic marketing needs.

Tom Lupo, National Sales Director
Noevir
Irvine, California

Networking has provided a constant source of business referrals, job opportunities, and close relationships with key individuals within the business community. Continual networking has opened many doors and avenues for me that would otherwise be closed.

Networking has given me the opportunity to meet new members who have led to a continual line of referrals and added friendships.

Paul Schultz, Membership Services
M.A.C.
Minneapolis, Minnesota

Networking activities helped to drive my management consulting business. We obtain leads and ideas from clients, former clients, prospects, and from all types of industry sources.

Networking for professional purposes allowed me to meet my wife. In addition, networking in the community, the church, and with service organizations has provided more benefits and much pleasure. It is impossible to calculate the financial benefits, but without networking, I would not be enjoying my current personal and business success.

Ray Larson, President
Larson Associates
Brea, California

Although I didn't have a title for it at the time, networking launched me into my teaching career just out of college, led me through two major career changes, and now into my current position as president of Weekenders Casual Wear, Inc. Networking has also been the method by which I have built Weekenders from ground floor to a multi-million dollar company. Examples of the fruits of networking are too numerous to count, but two stand out in my mind.

When I was ready to make my last career change, I set the networking process in motion and received a phone call from Canada one day. The owner of Weekenders in Canada was ready to start a Weekenders company in the U.S. He was calling me because of a business acquaintance of his who lived in the same apartment building as a friend of mine. They met while sharing a taxi one day and she told him about her direct-selling background. When George started looking for someone to start the U.S. operation his acquaintance recommended my friend who in turn gave him my name!

Months later, while chatting with a gentleman on the train to Chicago one day, I was given the name of a lady who he thought might be interested in joining our company. Not only did she do so, but she introduced another woman who became our top sales person and a sales manager. Gerry also introduced me to the lady who is our current director of sales development. So the positive effects of that conversation on the train go on and on in Weekenders!

Rosemary Redmond, President
Weekenders
Vernon Hills, Illinois

Networking for me is a way of life. And it is more from the heart than from the head. I find that by practicing networking communication from the heart, my entire business outlook has changed. It is a mutually beneficial process and has become my business. Never before have I been

more excited about what I do, because everyday I can see
how others are using the transfer of trust in their networking
environment to work for them. Now that's good business.

Relationships develop naturally from your network and
overlap into all facets of your life, enriching both your
personal and business areas. Regarding financial success,
forget about it! Help others attain it and become stronger.
As Anne says, "don't expect anything in return. Your
network will give back to you more than you ever expected."

As an entrepreneur, I could not effectively run my
business without the advice, support, services, products, and
positive vibes that I receive from my friends in my network.

Dan Doody, Marketing Coordinator
Network USA
Edina, Minnesota

The best networking is that which is genuine, sincere,
and not self-serving. Those for whom networking is a
natural extension of themselves are truly interested in other
people. They are genuinely curious about your business or
your personal being, and they touch base with you because
it is in their inherent nature to do so, out of respect for you
as an individual. Benefits accrue for these people because
they are imbued with personal responsibility and see the
world for he sum of its parts. The true winners, in my book,
are those who do not have to be taught how to network—it
is simply part of their nature.

Steve Bailey, President
The National Management Association
Dayton, Ohio

I have met the most intriguing speaking professionals.
Word of mouth is the only way for me to achieve the results
I need for my career. Networking is vital to someone like

myself who depends on the opinion and point-of-view of others.

Most of my speakers are also wonderful friends. In having such a wonderful business/personal connection with my speakers, the networking circle enlarges when other "friends" are introduced. There's a dual financial success story in my case. If a speaker is superb, I look good and this creates a win-win situation for both of us.

Debbie Hill, Education Coordinator
SHRM
Alexenderia, Virginia

My real estate business is a people business and if you do not come in contact with people effectively you won't be giving yourself the opportunity to succeed. As a branch sales manager my contacts are mostly with agents, both mine and other brokers whom I'm attempting to offer an opportunity to be more successful with Coldwell Banker.

By being involved in the local city chamber of commerce, Del Mar Merchants' Association, Kiwanis, Carmel Valley Merchants' Association, and parks and recreation departments, I am able to contribute to local activities and assist the community in accomplishing their objectives. I find this approach of networking in the community to be a low-key approach to recruiting and establishing a positive image for realtors in the community. It gets results!

Networking helps in all aspects of relationships by letting people know you care and are interested in the positive energy you as well as they have to give. Financially it helps to provide the confidence to those who are in the network who do business with my company or its agents. It has an overall positive effect on all aspects of your life.

Tom Ritchie, Branch Sales Manager
Coldwell Banker
Del Mar, California

Since learning how to become a successful networker, I have had numerous business opportunities available to me. By having a networking base, I have been able to take advantage of these opportunities.

Networking has opened me up to many people who were just waiting to talk to someone, but didn't know how. Once the ice was broken, I developed lots of new friends and built a networking base which has increased my business.

Henry L. Heller, President
Grand Postal Junction
West Hills, California

"Networking," at least certain aspects of it, was something I practiced early in my career in community college administration. Learning to work collaboratively with my colleagues was my motivation in those fledging years, and I found listening to be my most valuable tool. Opportunities to attend local, state, and national meetings provided more and more contacts with seasoned professionals: innovators, expert researchers and practitioners in the field of learning. My abilities to engage in productive exchange with such professionals seemed to grow, and I found follow-up communication by telephone and mail to be productive for both parties. I was discovering my own new approaches, an others were beginning to ask my advice, even to replicate some of those approaches on their own campuses. Because of these contacts, invitations to serve on important committees and commissions increased in number. Career advancement now seemed realistic, and, indeed, materialized. Should I have been told, at some point during those years, that I was "networking," I would have been puzzled. Like Anne Boe in her early career, "I was living the concept" without defining it.

Since retiring, I find that many of the rewarding professional relationships, developed over the years, continue to enrich my life. I continue to participate in my community.

My wife and I, and our daughter and three sons (and their families) continue to grow, and travel here and abroad, and it appears my "net" is still working!

Erv Metzgar
Grossmont-Cuyamaca Community College
El Cajon, California

Networking has been a dynamic vehicle for me to meet professionals and unconditionally give and receive information and services. Networking is a must personally and professionally it's the true giving of self in an information explosive, high paced society.

Personally, networking is a philosophy of living—a way of life to develop and sustain relationships. Like any skill, networking needs to be exercised daily, but I think everyone innately is a networker. It's whom we meet and "network" with that allows us to grow in all areas of our life. Networking is consistent and constant. The true test of its effectiveness is to ask yourself, "Who is in my life at the present moment and who do I want in my life always?"

Paul Davis, Public Relations Coordinator
San Diego County Credit Union
San Diego, California

Networking has helped my career advancement tremendously. I started my career at age sixteen working for the chamber of commerce. By having my first job in a public position, I learned how important networking was to accomplish business and personal goals. I learned that in order to get cooperation and participation, I needed to keep communication open with a variety of people always staying in touch. By networking, I have been able to move up my career ladder at a faster pace by introducing myself to key industry players and networking at social functions. I have also kept in touch with most of my previous employers. As an example, a few months ago I appeared on a video that was broadcast via satellite. I didn't have access to the broadcast, but I have kept a relationship with my old boss who did have access (I worked for her ten years ago) and was able to have her tape my session. If I hadn't kept in contact, I wouldn't have a copy of the video.

Networking has contributed a great deal to my relationships. Human relations are very important to me. I care about people and have a genuine love for humanity. Therefore, I make a point to keep in touch with everyone that I care about. Even if it is a short voice mail just to let them know I'm thinking of them. Because of this, I have a strong "support system" available to me in personal and professional life. Of course, I feel that networking has contributed not only to my financial success, but to the success of my being.

Elizabeth Hudson, Director of Marketing
Premenos Corporation
Concord, California

My career in community relations spans twenty years, and I can divide it into two stages: before networking, and after networking. Before I learned to be an effective networker, I was moderately successful. Now that networking is an integral part of every day, I'm phenomenally successful. Referrals are abundant. Both new accounts and public relations opportunities come my way unsolicited. All I do is play an active role in my community and what a great feeling it is to know I'm helping others meet their goals. All the new business that comes my way just happens.

I originally studied networking as it applied to one specific job, but I've found that it's a skill essential to all aspects of life: career, investing, relationships, and so on. Everyday I'm presented with interesting opportunities that, without the networking seeds planted months ago, would never have come my way. Networking is like a magic carpet ride to personal and financial success. And the best part is that I get to take all of my new friends with me.

Janeen Olsen, Community Relations Specialist
Entertainment Publications, Inc.
Portland, Oregon

Networking has helped me by expanding my opportunities from time to time. I found both a previous job and my current position through network contacts. I now find myself in a position with unlimited networking potential.

My dream career position came from a network contact and has afforded me financial growth potential. I've also recently started a new network by putting together an investment group of career women. My personal circle of friendships continues to grow through every networking opportunity I encounter.

Jackie Wilson, Executive Officer
Tallahassee Builders Association
Tallahassee, Florida

Networking is an invaluable resource to me as I negotiate day-to-day activities. It seems as though I find myself consulting with my network as often as I can. The individuals who comprise my network represent a pool of talent that becomes a reliable source of information to me.

Networking makes it possible for me to become acquainted with a variety of people. My interaction with the individuals in my network enhances my base of knowledge and it broadens the experience I have. I am able to become more effective in my role as a result of people in my network.

Dr. Richard Sanchez, President
Grossmont College
El Cajon, California

A sense of "community" and involvement in today's culture is critical to survival and the continued building of our society's self-esteem. Networking, as stressed by Anne Boe, is the cornerstone of a successful, fulfilling career, and is the most important contribution professionals can make toward attaining high quality communication in the business world. Today, apprehension and a question of trust in one another has forced our business environments to look at our commitment levels and the civility (or lack thereof) that we use in our relationships. The principles of networking have been a driving force in the success of my career and in my ability to value others for their unique influences on me.

Because networking is the transition point from mediocrity to peak performance, I have discovered that mastering that "one-on-one" relationship is responsible for the level of harmony and fulfillment that I find, today, in my personal and professional relationships. The idea of being focused on one another's needs is far more productive than approaching a relationship with conditional expectations. The wealth that I am experiencing in my life is more than financial—networking has allowed me to manifest a richness in quality of life and quality of relationships. Because of that richness and because of networking, I am personally making a more valuable contribution to our society.

Mary Ellen Bedri, Training Manager
Chase Manhattan
San Diego, California

As budding motivational speakers we set about establishing a network with some of the industry leaders like Mark Victor Hansen, Bob Harris, and Anne Boe. As a result of these contacts and their endorsements, we easily accelerated our career through five years of growth in only six months. Networking has been an invaluable tool. Our circle of contacts has grown exponentially as a result of it, and over the next year our personal incomes are expected to increase tenfold.

Networking is ABOUT relationships. We have discovered that successful networking results not only in good business but also in good relationships. Many of the people we have networked with have become dear and cherished friends. In fact there are few places we visit in North America that we don't run into some of these friends and we are eternally grateful for each and every one.

Ian T. May and Keith Laplante
Investors Group
Peterborough, Ontario Canada

Networking is my career. As the National President of the National Association for Professional Saleswomen, I have met and done business with women all across the country. Women make contacts, get sales leads and often get better jobs by making use of the networking contacts available through NAPS.

Personally, my financial success depends on networking. I am a headhunter and I need to find the "person who knows the person" I'm looking for on any job assignment. Through my networking efforts, I have friends and contacts in every major city in the United States.

Marie Houle, President
Quality Search
Saint Paul, Minnesota

In a "nutshell" - "It's not what you know that counts, It's who you know!" Networking is the best way to leverage the time and skills that put a limit on your success!!!

The size of my "Network" is directly proportional to the number of relationships and financial success that I have. I hope giving "can always be my top priority." Because in giving; I have received multifold on return. Most

importantly, "Never keep score when giving," you don't
need to!!! It works!!

> Don Craighead, Executive Officer
> DHC Enterprises, Inc.
> St. Paul, Minnesota

There is no sustained success in business and/or in
one's career without working with and through people.
Every interaction becomes a part of one's intricate network
of human relationships. Without this network, be it family
. . . immediate or extended, friends, colleagues, associates
and even casual aquaintances, my life and my career would
have been without meaning.

Networking has taught me that there is value in every
human relationship regardless of title or position. As a result
of my not prejudging a person's worth and opening my mind
and heart to their unique purpose, I have acquired riches
beyond my wildest dreams that are both spiritual and financial.

> George Fraser, President
> SuccessSource, Inc.
> Cleveland, Ohio

Author of   Success Runs in our Race -
            the complete guide to effective
            networking in the African American
            community.

BE A PEOPLE PERSON!

I have always been a people person, sometimes to a fault. Even
when "evil" is staring me in the face, I try to find some good in it.
This attitude has created a networking farm ground. When you are
looking for good in people, you tend to be more open to their ideas.
Believe me, some of the people I have been around, you need to
sift through a lot of idle chatter to get the good idea that they have
in their head.

Everybody has some useful ideas. It is just a matter of listening to them until you get them. Having the patience to get to the idea earns our repsect. You don't earn respect from peers if you brush them off. You get it by listening to their ideas, and helping them polish those ideas to help them reach their goals. That's what I am about.

I think that I touched on the relationship issue above. If you earn someone's respect, they may tell someone else about you and what you do. Networking helps relationships because you keep fresh ideas in your mind that you can pass on. Relationships are a two way street. You need to give, as well as receive.

As for financial success, it is a matter of time. Success is forthcoming! Through networking, some BIG doors will start to open up. Now, it is up to me to walk through those doors. It all started by just being willing to share ideas. At first, you tend to do more learning and searching. Always think about ways to improve on the idea and then create new ideas that you can then pass along to others. After you have been networking for awhile, you start giving as a way of life. Another new person comes along, and the cycle starts over.

Now, it's your turn to become a **notable networker.** Answer the same questions as the networkers above answered:

1. How has networking worked for you in your business and/or career? _____

_____

_____

_____

_____

_____

2. How has networking contributed to your relationships and financial success? _____

_____

_____

_____

_____

Congratulations! You are now a **notable networker** too. Continue to integrate the ideas expressed in this book on a daily basis. You will soon become unconsciously competent and your world will soon be filled with happiness, inner peace, and joy as you continue to help someone else make their dreams come true. Remember, what goes around comes around. Welcome home!

WINNING THE NEW NETWORKING GAME: KEEPING AHEAD OF THE BUSINESS WORLD

Networking is an exciting real-life adventure. It is for everyone who likes playing the game and winning. Networking is a game of self-discovery. Each time you are given an opportunity to make a move, take the risk. Take a chance you may discover hidden treasures within yourself. Even while the results of what you want to produce don't always happen immediately, the adventure can be rewarding and exciting.

"Come to the edge," he said.
They said: "We are afraid."
"Come to the edge," he said.
They came.
He pushed them . . . and they flew!
                                        — Guillaume Apollinaire

Networking is a pleasure that guarantees that anyone who partakes with a win-win attitude will be a guaranteed winner. In other words, what you put in, you will get back. You never know how the intricate maze of connections and interactions may one day loop around to support you on your particular path. Enjoy the trip — I think you are terrific!

HAPPY NETWORKING!

ANNE BOE'S
NETWORKING SUCCESS TOOLS

Learn How to Increase Your Net-Worth, Romantic Possibilities & Career Opportunities Now!

1. **Book—Is Your Net-Working?** $25.00
   - How to develop your networking plan
   - How to communicate with effectiveness and power
   - Networking in the 1990s and beyond

2. **Video—1 hour—"Networking For Your Personal and Financial Growth"** ... $40.00
   - How to follow up your business contacts
   - How to turn rolodex cards into money
   - Setting goals—taking action—getting results

3. **Video—1 hour—"How To Net Your Playmate"** $30.00
   - How to overcome your fear of rejection
   - How to strengthen your dating confidence
   - How to attract the right people

4. **Cassette Tape Program—3 hours—"Is Your Net-Working?"** $25.00
   - How to network for customer services and sales success
   - How to integrate the 29 keys to successful networking
   - How to work smarter, not harder

5. **Anne Boe's Getahead™ Software Program (IBM compatible)** $55.00
   - How to track and nurture your network
   - How to keep connected to your business contacts
   - How to increase sales and customer service

6. **New Book—"Networking Success: How to Turn Business & Financial Relationships into Fun & Profit"** $14.95
   - How to turn networking into net-worthing
   - How to strengthen your intuition and trust yourself
   - How to create all win-win relationships

7. **Networking Success—6 Audio Cassettes and Book** $69.00
   - How to integrate networking throughout your life
   - How to increase business success and visibility
   - How to develop winning career strategies

8. **Successful Women in Network Marketing Video** $30.00
   - How to empower yourself in your business relationships
   - How to increase your self-confidence and well-being
   - How to create more wealth through networking

(California Residents add 7.75% tax.)
Toll Free VISA/MASTERCARD—1-800-484-9914 (Code 5609). Fax 619-942-6878.
(Add $3.50 Shipping & Handling. Add $5.00 for Software.)

Name: _____ Phone: (   )_____

Address:_____

City, State, Zip: _____

(CHECK)   (VISA)   (MASTERCARD)   Total Purchase: _____

Card #_____ Expiration Date:_____

HCI's Business Self-Help Books Motivate and Inspire

The Master Motivator
Secrets of Inspiring Leadership
Mark Victor Hansen and Joe Batten

Today's competitive economic climate demands managers who can lead and inspire. Here is the definitive book on motivating others from two of the world's most renowned and respected motivational speakers. Joe Batten—mentor to Ross Perot and author of *Tough-Minded Management*—and Mark Victor Hansen—motivator/ communicator extraordinaire and co-author of the bestselling *Chicken Soup for the Soul* series—show you how to achieve top performance from yourself and those you lead: you can become *The Master Motivator*. An empowering book that will be on the must-read list of every executive and manager in America.
Code 3553 . . . . $9.95

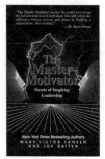

Going Public
A Practical Guide to Developing Personal Charisma
Hal Milton

Risk-taking is key to achieving success in many areas of life, from business ventures to personal relationships. Yet often we fail to reach our goals because fear paralyzes us. This inspiring book is a step-by-step guide to overcoming the fear of any type of performance, developing authentic communication and increasing self-expression. Author Hal Milton uses exercises and experiences derived from his proven STAR performance training workshops while incorporating examples from sports psychology, entertainment, business and other performance arenas. After reading this book, you'll soar to new heights on the wings of renewed strength and creativity.
Code 360X $9.95

What You Want, Wants You
How to Get Out of Your Rut
Debra Jones

People in the 1990s are reevaluating their lifestyles as never before. With the stability of tenured positions in large corporations becoming a thing of the past, many workers are rethinking their career choices to be more in tune with what they really want to do. Here, Debra Jones, marketing whiz extraordinaire, gives you a game plan for digging yourself out of the quagmire of indecision and hopelessness in order to find your life path. An inspiring book that will leave you revitalized.
Code 3677 . . . . $9.95

The Art of the Fresh Start
How to Make and Keep Your New Year's Resolutions for a Lifetime
Glenna Salsbury

In the #1 *New York Times* bestseller *Chicken Soup for the Soul*, Glenna Salsbury told her inspiring story of miraculously seeing her dreams become reality. Now she shares with you her practical, step-by-step approach for tapping into your core being in order to achieve permanent, repeatable and ongoing self-renewal. This unique approach to goal-setting through internal and spiritual guidance will teach you to live a life filled with hope, joy and a multitude of fresh starts.
Code 3642 . . . . $9.95

Available at your favorite bookstore or call 1-800-441-5569 for Visa or MasterCard orders.
Prices do not include shipping and handling. Your response code is HCI.

HCI's Business Self-Help Books Motivate and Inspire

The Master Motivator
Secrets of Inspiring Leadership
Mark Victor Hansen and Joe Batten

Today's competitive economic climate demands managers who can lead and inspire. Here is the definitive book on motivating others from two of the world's most renowned and respected motivational speakers. Joe Batten—mentor to Ross Perot and author of *Tough-Minded Management*—and Mark Victor Hansen—motivator/communicator extraordinaire and co-author of the bestselling *Chicken Soup for the Soul* series—show you how to achieve top performance from yourself and those you lead: you can become *The Master Motivator*. An empowering book that will be on the must-read list of every executive and manager in America.

Code 3553 .... $9.95

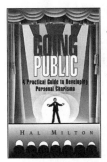

Going Public
A Practical Guide to Developing Personal Charisma
Hal Milton

Risk-taking is key to achieving success in many areas of life, from business ventures to personal relationships. Yet often we fail to reach our goals because fear paralyzes us. This inspiring book is a step-by-step guide to overcoming the fear of any type of performance, developing authentic communication and increasing self-expression. Author Hal Milton uses exercises and experiences derived from his proven STAR performance training workshops while incorporating examples from sports psychology, entertainment, business and other performance arenas. After reading this book, you'll soar to new heights on the wings of renewed strength and creativity.

Code 360X $9.95

What You Want, Wants You
How to Get Out of Your Rut
Debra Jones

People in the 1990s are reevaluating their lifestyles as never before. With the stability of tenured positions in large corporations becoming a thing of the past, many workers are rethinking their career choices to be more in tune with what they really want to do. Here, Debra Jones, marketing whiz extraordinaire, gives you a game plan for digging yourself out of the quagmire of indecision and hopelessness in order to find your life path. An inspiring book that will leave you revitalized.

Code 3677 .... $9.95

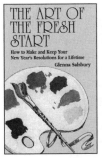

The Art of the Fresh Start
How to Make and Keep Your New Year's Resolutions for a Lifetime
Glenna Salsbury

In the #1 *New York Times* bestseller *Chicken Soup for the Soul*, Glenna Salsbury told her inspiring story of miraculously seeing her dreams become reality. Now she shares with you her practical, step-by-step approach for tapping into your core being in order to achieve permanent, repeatable and ongoing self-renewal. This unique approach to goal-setting through internal and spiritual guidance will teach you to live a life filled with hope, joy and a multitude of fresh starts.

Code 3642 .... $9.95

Available at your favorite bookstore or call 1-800-441-5569 for Visa or MasterCard orders.
Prices do not include shipping and handling. Your response code is HCI.

Share the Magic of Chicken Soup

Lift Your Spirits with
Chicken Soup for the Soul Audiotapes

World-renowned inspirational speakers Jack Canfield and Mark Victor Hansen share stories from their two *New York Times* bestsellers *Chicken Soup for the Soul* and *A 2nd Helping of Chicken Soup for the Soul* on these heartwarming audiotapes.

The Best of the Original Chicken Soup for the Soul Audiotape

This single 90-minute cassette contains the very best stories from the ABBY award-winning *Chicken Soup for the Soul.* You will be enlightened and entertained by the masterful storytelling of Jack and Mark and friends. The essential stories are all here.

Code 3723: One 90-minute audiocassette $9.95

Chicken Soup for the Soul Audio Gift Set

This six-tape set includes the entire audio collection of stories from *Chicken Soup for the Soul*, over seven hours of listening pleasure. The inspirational message spoken in this set will not only enhance your commute to and from work, it will also leave you in a positive frame of mind the whole day. Listen to these tapes at home and be uplifted by the insights and wisdom of these emotionally powerful stories. A wonderful gift for friends, loved ones or yourself.

Code 3103: Six cassettes—7 hours of inspiration . . $29.95

A 2nd Helping of Chicken Soup for the Soul Abridged Version Audiotape

The newest collection of *Chicken Soup* stories, straight from the sequel. This two-tape volume brings to you the authors' favorite stories from *A 2nd Helping of Chicken Soup for the Soul.* Now you can listen to the newest batch in your car or in the comfort of your own home. Fresh stories to brighten your day!

Code 3766: Two 90-minute cassettes $14.95

Available at your favorite bookstore or call 1-800-441-5569 for Visa or MasterCard orders. Prices do not include shipping and handling. Your response code is HCI.

STORY BOOKS TO ENLIGHTEN AND ENTERTAIN

Catch the Whisper of the Wind
Collected Stories and Proverbs from Native Americans
Cheewa James

The richness of Native American culture is explored by noted motivational speaker and broadcast journalist Cheewa James. These provocative stories touch the heart and offer deep insight into the soul of the Indian.

Code 3693 ....$9.95

The 7th Floor Ain't Too High for Angels to Fly
A Collection of Stories on Relationships and Self-Understanding
John M. Eades, Ph.D.

In this diverse collection of provocative stories, therapist John Eades helps readers to reflect on how they are living their own lives and invites them to discover the inner resources that lead to true joy and fulfillment. You'll laugh and cry, but you won't be able to put down *The 7th Floor Ain't Too High for Angels to Fly.*

Code 3561 ....$10.95

Bedtime Stories for Grown-ups
Fairy-Tale Psychology
Sue Gallehugh, Ph.D. and Allen Gallehugh

In this witty, fully illustrated book, therapist Sue Gallehugh and her son Allen adapt classic fairy tales to illustrate the fundamental principles of self-love through mental health and psychological growth. This upbeat, entertaining book will leave readers laughing out loud as they explore the value of the serious concept of self-worth.

Code 3618 ....$9.95

Values from the Heartland
Stories of an American Farmgirl
Bettie B. Youngs, Ph.D., Ed.D

One of the best-loved authors from *Chicken Soup for the Soul* shares uplifting, heartwarming tales, culled from her memories of growing up on a farm in Iowa. These value-laden stories will show you how hard times, when leavened with love and support, can provide strength of character, courage and leadership.

Code 3359: paperback $11.95
Code 3340: hard cover $22.00

Mentors, Masters and Mrs. MacGregor
Stories of Teachers Making a Difference
Jane Bluestein, Ph.D.

Jane Bluestein asked celebrities and common folks around the world the following question: Who is that one special teacher that made a difference in your life? The collected answers to this question make up this truly touching book which will appeal to the student—and the teacher—in all of us.

Code 3375: paperback $11.95
Code 3367: hard cover $22.00

Available at your favorite bookstore or call 1-800-441-5569 for Visa or MasterCard orders. Prices do not include shipping and handling. Your response code is HCI.